Yount on Agency Management

by
Lewis C. Yount, CLU

FARNSWORTH PUBLISHING COMPANY, INC.
Rockville Centre, NY 11570

Published by Farnsworth Publishing Co., Inc.
Rockville Centre, New York 11570.
Library of Congress Catalog Card No. 84-80275.
ISBN 0-87863-190-9.
Manufactured in the United States of America.

DEAR BILL,
CONGRATULATIONS ON WINNING THE PRESIDENT'S TROPHY! PAGES 15 & 16 OF THIS BOOK TELL HOW I FEEL ABOUT YOUR MAGNIFICENT RECORD. BEST WISHES FOR CONTINUED GOOD HEALTH, HAPPINESS & SUCCESS.
Lew Yount 3-21-84

This book is dedicated to my wife, Grace, in appreciation of her nearly 40 years of support and encouragement. Also, special appreciation is given to my daughter, Nancy Kay Dodge, for her expertise with the word processor which made my penmanship legible for the publisher.

PREFACE

Some twenty years ago a friend who had a solid home office position told me this story: He had been waiting in the chairman's anteroom for nearly an hour to discuss a matter of some consequence to the company when there was a clatter down the hall and in walked the company's leading general agent, surrounded by a couple of supervisors. "Tell the Old Man I'm here, sweetie," he said to the chairman's secretary. Almost immediately the door opened and the general agent and his entourage swept in.

"I waited another hour," said my friend, "and then I decided to apply for a general agency."

That was 20 years ago. The general agent or manager, if he was successful, was king. But times have changed. Managers and general agents are now part of the marketing team. It isn't that they are less important. They are still irreplaceable. But career managers today recognize far more than ever before that they cannot do it alone. The up-to-date products that only the actuaries can design are a must. The sophisticated computer backup with all the sales and service advantages it provides requires home office involvement and almost always home office money as well. High agent financing requirements likewise.

The life insurance business as it expands into these products and services, has become lean and mean where it used to be comparatively fat and sweet; under the circumstances there was no other choice. As a result, strictures being placed on field organization have never been tighter. An agency must either become productive and profitable or the company has two alternatives: replace the manager with someone they hope can get the job done or merge the agency with another better managed operation.

Despite all this, I have the firm belief that agency management is the most challenging and rewarding job in the life insurance business. I'd never have any other.

This book is my testament. It tells you why I became an agency manager and why I was happy for 30 years being one.

But it presumes to go beyond that: It undertakes to tell today's aspiring managers some of the things they can do to make the job as rewarding as I found it. I have a lot of suggestions for them, and every one of these suggestions has worked *for me.*

This book also is my philosophy. You won't find in it any time-control charts or tables of organization. I will leave those esoteric things to my friends at the Life Insurance Marketing and Research Association. I believe that a person without a sound philosophy of life and life insurance will never reach his potential until he acquires one. It's my profound hope that this book will give people in the life insurance business—and, yes, the financial service business—a broader base on which to construct their own philosophies.

As I have read the proofs of this book, I find that I apologized only once for the extensive use of masculine pronouns. Perhaps this is natural: During my career the role of agency manager has been almost exclusively masculine. But for those young women who are aspiring to management jobs, let me say: Turn the pronouns around anytime they suit you, and I will be happy.

INTRODUCTION

My first contacts with Lew Yount came in 1966-67, when he was president of the National Association of Life Underwriters and I was agency officer for the New England Life. I was impressed by the precise way he handled this most formidable of field positions, accomplishing the countless tasks of an NALU head without ever seeming ruffled either by the job or maintaining the position of a preeminent manager for the Prudential. If the phrase "laid back" had been in vogue then, he would have epitomized it.

After I moved to LIMRA, I grew to know him more as a field manager, and once more I was impressed by what I saw. He was a member of the Research Agencies Group which had been established by LIMRA. This was the precursor of hundreds of groups that exist today where outstanding managers and general agents compare their experiences, contribute to each others' banks of information and prepare extensive research projects on subjects of common interest.

Lew was one of the leaders of the Research Agencies Group. After a time he began to contribute some of his thoughts to *Managers Magazine,* a LIMRA publication, and his comments about agency management proved to be among the most popular articles ever to appear in it. Some of them have been expanded for publication in this book.

My admiration stems in part from the balance he has always shown in his business life with Prudential and his public contribution to NALU and the General Agents and Managers Conference, which he also headed. To be able to control one of the top agencies in the top company while contributing substantially to the general good of the profession isn't an easy task, as anyone who has tried it knows. But Lew Yount made it look easy.

The reader will find this book unusual for its total frankness. Lew spends more time than most people in self-analysis, and his estimates of what he would do differently another time around should be must reading for agency heads and those who are contemplating such a career. This is by no means a textbook; rather it is a searching inquiry into the factors that lead to both success and failure.

In my opinion, Lewis C. Yount has added significantly to the literature of agency management. His realism should be a refreshing draught at the well of wisdom for agency heads and those who aspire to be.

—George G. Joseph, CLU
President Emeritus
Life Insurance Marketing and Research Association

CONTENTS

1.

WHY BECOME AN AGENCY HEAD?

This book has been put together not only for those who presently occupy managerial positions, but also to show the way to others who may be considering careers in management.

Ten years ago, this initial chapter would not have been as pertinent as it is today. There was a time when many agents looked upon the job of agency head as the capstone of their careers. But several things have happened in the interim which make many managerial candidates pause and reflect on their futures. For instance:

- As the cost squeeze racks the home offices, they in turn put the squeeze on their field units. The call today is for greater efficiency and more productivity. The person who has any doubts about his capacity to learn how to perform effectively the necessary managerial functions would do well to stay away from a management career. But to the person who is both efficient and productive, managing an agency may hold a greater challenge and greater rewards than at any time in the history of the life insurance business.

- Some companies are undertaking to bring into being a new breed of managers: men and women who have sharpened their managerial skills—perhaps in business unrelated to life insurance—but have never exhibited any sales skills. This experiment hasn't yet proved out and may never do so. In my view, the rapport between an agency head and his agents depends, as you will see throughout this book, on a thorough understanding of the many and varied problems of the agent. It will take a professional manager with no sales experience a long time to achieve the empathy with his people that the person who has come up through the ranks feels immediately.

- Many companies have begun to turn to the personal producing general agent (PPGA) as the solution for their marketing problems. This may work in small communities where a single person, operating with a small staff, can maintain the company's share of market. But it is a wasteful procedure in, say, the country's 200 largest cities where a large agency force is required to keep the company both visible and profitable. The idea of paying general agents' overrides to all members of the field force is about as inefficient and expensive as a company operation can be. So there will always be room for the agency manager in the leading communities.

MY PERSONAL EXPERIENCES

Managing a life insurance agency was the best job in the world for me. I enjoyed the work and the challenge that goes with it right up to the day I retired at age 65. I never seriously considered any of the numerous home office positions I was offered by Prudential and other companies. Some of them were quite attractive and, assuming I had performed satisfactorily, my net income probably would have been substantially greater. Neither did I ever seriously consider retiring early, although Prudential's pension plan makes retirement a viable alternative to working when one reaches age 60 and has at least 30 years of service.

The reasons I chose to make a career of managing an agency might not necessarily be the same as those you might use in making such a decision. But I believe the reasons which attracted me to the job are just as valid today as they were 31 years ago in spite of all the changes that have taken place. All of us are different. We march to different drummers. However, spelling out as specifically as I can why I became a manager and remained one for 30 years will give others some guidelines for making an intelligent decision as to whether or not it is the career for them. In addition. I will include some observations, pro and con, about various aspects of the job which will be helpful.

When I first entered the insurance business as an agent for Prudential in the Seattle agency in April of 1946, management was the farthest thing from my mind. I was told that I could make a good living if I sold enough insurance and I made the commitment to work as hard and as long as it took to become successful. After a couple of years as an agent, I knew I could make it selling life insurance.

I was challenged to enter management by the agency manager. I became a supervisor with a mutual understanding that I would "try" it for two years, and if it did not work out satisfactorily for both of us, I would resume my career as an agent. It is interesting that I never moved to Tacoma where the detached office I was managing was located. I stayed in Olympia, which was about 35 miles from the office. I continued to write a fair amount of business in Olympia while doing some recruiting and training in Tacoma. If management did not work out, I was keeping myself in good position to resume my career as an agent. In fact, I was about ready to do just that when Prudential offered me the job of regional manager in the Western Home Office in Los Angeles, working with the ordinary agency managers in that territory. It took me a month to decide between moving to L.A. or resigning my supervisor's position, staying in Olympia and concentrating on personal production. I knew I couldn't go on managing an office 35 miles away and I did not want to move to Tacoma. I finally made the decision to move to L.A. and after about three years came back to Seattle as agency manager.

It was while I was working with the various managers in the West, a number of whom had managed agencies for Prudential for many years, that I became excited about the job and decided it was what I wanted to do with my life. I am giving you all of this personal background so you will know where I was coming from when I was appointed manager of the Seattle Agency on September 1, 1952.

As I visited these various agencies, I became good friends with several senior Prudential managers, all of whom were old enough to be my father. They were all different and it was a real education for me to talk with them and ask them questions. It was through my exposure to these wonderful gentlemen that I learned what a rewarding lifetime career managing an agency could be. There were a number of factors which influenced my thinking, all of which were interrelated and all important.

HELPING PEOPLE DEVELOP

One thing that I found very appealing was the special opportunity the manager has to play a key role in helping other people develop. There is tremendous personal satisfaction in bringing young people into the business and helping them to grow and mature as human beings and life insurance people. If I were to select one reason above all others for becoming a manager, this would be it. If you can visualize yourself as finding real enjoyment and a psychological reward that money cannot buy through success in this aspect of the job, then this is probably the most compelling reason to consider a management career.

While working on this chapter I had occasion to talk with Bill Quiring who manages Prudential's San Francisco Agency. I was instrumental in bringing Bill into the business in 1957 as an agent in the Seattle Agency. He was a very successful agent and an excellent supervisor. He spent a total of 15 years in our agency—4 as an agent and 11 as a supervisor. He could have been a manager sooner but was doing well where he was, and didn't like the potential of the agencies he was offered. In 1972, the Western Home Office took him into the training department with my blessing and with the understanding that he would be made a manager in a good area within a year. In April of 1973, he was appointed manager of the San Francisco Agency. There were several good agents in the agency at the time but it was by no means a plum. Bill has done a magnificent job of recruiting and retention during the past 10 years and in 1983 his agency was the #1 ordinary agency in Prudential.

Bill did not have a great deal going for him when he joined our agency—high school education only, no market, and his financial condition left something to be desired. But he was, and is, a highly motivated, quality person and the life insurance business gave him the opportunity to demonstrate what his capabilities were. To say the least, I am proud to have played a part in his development.

There are numerous other individuals in the Seattle Agency, as well as former members of the agency, who have made remarkable progress. It would be a pleasure to write about each one of them because of the satisfaction it gives me to know that I played some part in their growth and development. I hope those former associates who read this will accept my choice of Bill Quiring for special attention because of the current recognition which came to him, and properly so, as the result of his agency's outstanding production in 1983.

The only reason I am able to enjoy the special feeling of empathy I have with Bill Quiring's success is because I was the agency manager who was part of his early struggles to become established both as an agent and as a supervisor. There are countless career managers and general agents who have enjoyed similar experiences and who know exactly what I am talking about. As I stated above, if the possibility of having this kind of experience "turns you on" then you should seriously consider becoming a manager.

HAVING ONE'S OWN BUSINESS

Something else that appealed to me about becoming an agency head was the opportunity to have my own business. Of course, agency managers and general agents have vice presidents to whom they report as well as budgetary restraints when they are using company money, as most of them are. But it has been my experience that successful agency heads are given considerable latitude and, as long as they do not stray too far from established company policies, they have the privilege of running their agencies very much as they would their own business. The Prudential permitted me to do that and I enjoyed the responsibility and challenge. It is true that agents too can build organizations, and many of them do, but their success will generally be determined in large measure by their personal efforts as contrasted with the manager who must achieve success by working through others.

If you are an agent to whom the idea of building a sizable organization with several staff people reporting to you as well as a goodly number of agents appeals, then you should consider agency management. Of course, whenever one is working with people there will be problems and the more people you have the more problems you will have. You will need considerable patience and understanding to cope with the many problems with which you will be faced. So you should examine your tolerance level in this area. Personally I found it a challenge. Although there were many occasions when I became frustrated, the occasional time when I was able to make a meaningful contribution made it all worthwhile.

Perhaps you would have the same reaction. You can probably evaluate how you will respond to these situations by analyzing how you have handled human relations problems to which you have been exposed in the past.

Successful managers work with people a great deal on a one-on-one basis. This includes in-office training as well as field coaching and joint selling. Of course, as the agency grows they may have supervisors to whom they can delegate most of these responsibilities. But initially, and to a certain extent on an ongoing basis, they should be involved in all of them. Effective year-end planning and goal-setting meetings with both supervisors and agents are critical to a manager's success. These are time consuming but their importance cannot be overestimated. There is a great deal of personal satisfaction, however, in working with people one-on-one in all of these situations. If you can project yourself enjoying this part of the manager's job, you have still another reason to consider a career in management.

RECRUITING—THE ALL-IMPORTANT JOB

Any consideration of becoming a manager would not be complete without some serious thinking about the all-important job of recruiting. It has been my experience that top agents do not find prospecting an insurmountable problem. Why? Because they have well-established prospecting methods which they work at *consistently.* Recruiting for the manager is very similar to prospecting for the agent. Recruiting sources and methods are common knowledge. I cannot recall when I have heard a really new recruiting idea. To be a successful recruiter requires that the manager work at it consistently just as the agent must do at prospecting, using an established procedure. Such a procedure can be developed from books and other material that are readily available. The Agency Management Training Course has some outstanding ideas and suggestions and I recommend it highly.

Personally, I never found recruiting to be a problem. As an agency we worked at it all the time and, as a result, invariably reached our annual recruiting goals. I enjoyed talking with prospective agents about the insurance business. I was always aware that the person with whom I was talking right then and there could become another multimillion dollar producer. And I found that exciting.

If you are conscious of the absolute necessity of continuous prospecting for an agent and are confident of your ability in this key activity, you can become a good recruiter. Recruiting and prospecting are not basically *mental* activities; they also require such *physical action* as picking up the phone and using it and getting out of the office to go see people. If you enjoy doing this and can discipline yourself to doing it consistently, you should not hesitate to become a manager because of anything you may have heard about the difficulty of recruiting. Our business has a tremendous opportunity for the right people and there are still plenty of them out there waiting receptively to hear our story. I have always believed that and I still do.

THE PRESTIGE OF THE TITLE

There is a certain amount of prestige that goes with the title. But this doesn't last long unless you are successful! In my early years as a manager I never gave it much thought. But after I achieved a fair degree of success, I would be less than candid if I were to say I didn't enjoy the recognition that came to me as a *successful* Prudential manager. Unquestionably, the general public tends to be impressed more by people who are called managers. And if this appeals to you—and you wouldn't be human if it didn't—this is another reason to become a manager. *Within* the industry, as we all know, outstanding personal producers are more highly respected by everyone than people from just about any other group. But the public is different; they go for titles.

This is not a very important reason for wanting to become a manager. But it is an understandable one and if you feel you measure up pretty well in the other areas and you find the idea of being called the manager attractive, it probably makes good sense for you to take a serious look at a management career.

WHY NOT TO BE A MANAGER

There are two very good reasons not to become a manager. The first has to do with money. Although successful managers are well compensated, successful agents are also well compensated, if not more so. In addition, there are many expenses of various types which the agency manager must assume and there is a current tendency for home offices to ask managers to pay for more and more of the sales aids and services that are needed to do the job. However, even though this increases their costs, successful managers do quite well financially and there is no reason to expect that to change. The home offices need people to manage their agencies and they have no choice but to make certain they are compensated fairly and adequately.

Another reason not to become a manager is if you somehow have the opinion that it is an easy way to make a better than average income. Obviously, I have not worked at many other jobs and none for a long period of time. But I can attest to the fact that at no time in my 30 years did I feel I had an easy job. It was a challenging job, very interesting and rewarding, but easy it was not. I believe you would find that managers throughout the industry would give a similar response if asked if they thought running an agency was an easy way to make a living.

As I have stated several times, I enjoyed being an agency manager. I must admit there were times when I found the work and responsibility more enjoyable than I did at other times. But, on balance, it was an enjoyable vocation for me. And I still think it is a great career for the right person.

I have tried in this chapter to be as objective as possible in addressing the question—why become an agency head? Hopefully, it has been helpful to some of the readers of this book.

There is another powerful reason, however, why you might be attracted to the career. It isn't something that can be analyzed and dissected. For want of a better way of expressing it, let's say it is just "something you want to do." If that feeling is strong within you, and you believe you are reasonably well qualified, and you are prepared to commit yourself to an all-out effort, I say go for it! You may find you will love the work as much as I did.

Furthermore, in so doing, you will become a part of what George Joseph, former President of LIMRA, has often referred to as the "most valuable asset in any life insurance company's investment portfolio." At the same time, you will become good friends, as I did, with the finest group of people you are ever likely to know—your fellow managers and general agents.

* * *

2.

WHY MANAGERS SUCCEED

Does anyone *really* know why agency managers succeed? If it turns out that one person does—and he can explain the reasons lucidly—several hundred agency officers who have the responsibility of selecting agency heads will beat a path to his door. And listening carefully in the background will be the senior officers of agency-building companies who are currently bedeviled by the ever-rising costs of agency operation.

I'm not the one with all the answers, I assure you. But I do have some ideas based on two things: my own 35 years of involvement in this field, and my friendship with a large number of outstanding general agents and managers in the United States and Canada. The latter is most important to me: I have visited their agencies, heard them speak and conduct workshops at industry meetings and listened to them present papers at LIMRA Research Agencies Group sessions for 14 years. It's their voices you will hear in the opinions that follow, as well as mine.

It seems to me that managers have three possibilities before them. They can either fail, survive or succeed. Failure tends to be final—one company at a time, perhaps. Just to survive, important as it is, is unrewarding and frustrating. Unfortunately, there are a large number of agency managers who appear to fall into that category. I would hope that the ideas in this chapter will help some who are just "surviving" to become successful.

"Success" is what we all want. But what is success to an agency head? Certainly there are no common criteria which are generally accepted. Qualifying for the National Management Award sponsored by the General Agents and Managers Conference would constitute success in some companies. In others it might not be good enough for the manager to hold his job. Furthermore, success means different things to different people as well as to different companies. Our goals and motivations are not the same.

In order for us to start on common ground, I suggest we use the following three points as a basis for determining if an agency head is successful:

1. The home office is satisfied.
2. The manager's spouse is satisfied.
3. The manager, himself, is "reasonably" satisfied. (This is the toughest one.)

If all three of these requirements are met, we should have a successful manager—and probably a happy one as well.

In talking with numerous home office agency people I have discovered that it is easier for them to explain the reasons why one manager failed than it is for them to explain why another one is successful. In fact, I have heard agency vice presidents say these exact words: "You know, I really don't know why so-and-so is so darn successful at running an agency. I just know that he is!" I would suggest that the reasons for success may be more subtle while the reasons for failure tend to be fairly obvious. "Success"—real success—comes about more slowly.

1. THE MANAGEMENT "STYLE"

So let us consider the first and most important reason why I think managers succeed—**They develop a "management style,"** to use a modern phrase, **and they are both consistent and persistent in following it.**

Let's examine that word "style" for a moment, because it means many things to many people. Most dictionaries take a column to define it. In this context, my favorite definition is "a particular, distinctive or characteristic mode of action."

Through the years I have read articles and heard talks by outstanding general agents and managers in which they told about their agencies. Many times my reaction was, "I couldn't do that or be like that." And it used to frustrate me. I felt there must be something wrong with me that I couldn't understand and accept what was obviously a very successful method of operating—for somebody else! Finally, it dawned on me that I had a style of my own and it had worked quite well for many years. It wasn't necessary for me to change my style. Make minor adjustments and changes, of course, but for the most part stay with what had worked, and was still working insofar as basic systems were concerned. The day I realized this was one of the happiest of my business career.

A. Recruiting

Here are some specific examples that reflect style. At the top of the list is recruiting. It takes quality people if an agency is to be successful and the only way to build such an organization is through quality recruiting. It cannot be done with radar or mirrors. It takes good old-fashioned work on a consistent basis. Successful managers develop definite recruiting procedures. They are fully aware of the absolute necessity of bringing new people into the agnecy. It has top priority on their agenda, almost on a daily basis.

There is really nothing new that can be said about recruiting sources. Anyone who has been involved in agency management for even a short period of time can write down an adequate list. The problem quite often is that the manager is looking for an "easy way." I don't believe there is one. At least if there is I never found it. Referrals from present organization probably comes the closest. But that does not just happen. The manager has to work at it and earn it!

The successful manager, however, has a recruiting system that works for him. He isn't looking for a new idea. He knows that all he has to do is work his system on a consistent basis and the results will come. The manager who is always seeking new recruiting ideas is, in my opinion, failure prone.

Present organization, warm nominators, cold nominators, policyholders, etc., are sources of prospective recruits with which all of us are familiar. Personal observation and contacts as well as seminar recruiting can be very productive. And don't overlook newspaper advertising. It is my personal experience that advertising for agents is a great deal like cold canvassing by an agent. It's unprofessional, it's undignified —but it works! Some of the best agents in my agency answered an ad, so I speak from experience.

The successful manager has a system of recruiting which *works for him*—which fits his "style"—and he works at it consistently. That is one of the key reasons he or she is successful.

B. Types of Agents

Secondly, these successful managers or general agents have pretty definite ideas regarding the type of agent who will fit into their organization. They want agents who will be receptive to their supervision, their marketing strategy and will readily be accepted by their present associates. In other words, they are looking for people who will complement and be comfortable with their style of agency management.

Let me give you a couple of examples of what I mean. Let us assume that the manager is a graduate of one of the top universities in the country. He might have his MBA or Law degree. He represents a company whose marketing strategy is to penetrate the peak market. The agency has the financing plan, supervision and backup support to introduce new people successfully into this market. The manager does not believe in sales campaigns—believes they are unprofessional. Obviously, this manager, to be successful, should be seeking well-educated potential recruits, preferably with good to excellent markets among upper income people, most of whom would probably be in their 30s or even older, with backgrounds in other professional or business fields.

Now let us consider a manager who represents a company which prefers to do business with a broader spectrum of the total market. His education may be limited to high school or junior college. He has always been highly interested in all forms of athletics, is a very competitive type and thoroughly enjoys promoting and participating in sales campaigns. His company's financing plan demands that new agents have a fast start by writing many applications. It is obvious that this manager will be successful with an entirely different type of agent. They can be younger with less formal education. A good market, although important, will not be as necessary. The relatively young, intense, competitive individual will probably fit in well with this manager's management style.

The two hypothetical agencies I have described above (or reasonable facsimiles) exist in every major city in the United States. In fact, in most cities of any size there are several of each type as well as numerous others with many of the characteristics of one or the other. But only a few of the agencies are successful as we have defined success. **They are the ones whose managers fully understand and accept what they have to work with and what their companies expect them to accomplish. They also understand themselves—their own strong points and limitations—as well as those of their super-**

visory staff. They know the type of agents they want and need for them to build a successful agency for the company they represent and they spend the time and effort necessary to attract these people to their agency in adequate numbers. Furthermore, they know from experience what selection standards, tests, and procedures work *for them.* And they use them religiously.

C. Supervisory and Motivation Techniques

Thirdly, the successful managers have well-established supervisory and motivational techniques which they follow consistently.

In the more sophisticated agency the tendency will be to use knowledge, tax information, etc., as a motivational tool. Workshops will be held on these subjects with discussions as to how to approach prospects in those fields. Supervisors will work with new agents both in the office and field on advanced cases—mostly a two interview or more sales process. Excellent backup services and assistance are available. Agents will be encouraged to become more and more knowledgeable and motivated to sell larger and larger policies. An increasing percentage of the agency's commissions will come from equity products and other nontraditional life insurance products of one kind or another.

The highly sophisticated agency manager may decide to go the full way into financial planning, and urge on his agents the ChFC or CFP designations. But he would do well to study the pitfalls of this road in some depth before he concludes that it is part of his style.

In the less sophisticated agency there will still be an emphasis on writing applications of all kinds and sizes. Activity will be closely supervised (calls, interviews, closing interviews, sales). Sales campaigns will be used on a fairly regular basis to recognize the leaders in apps as well as production.

Multiline activity will be permitted and in some companies encouraged. There will be some commissions earned from equity products. However, the preponderance of the agency's paid commissions will come from traditional life products.

Many agencies of these general types exist and with certain variations there are countless others. Once again the successful manager understands what *his style* is, the type of associate he is working with as well as the limitations and opportunities with the company he represents. He knows what has to be done and consistently does it. He rarely gets off track, but if, by chance, he should temporarily do so, he wastes no time getting back on it.

D. Training Schedules and Systems

Fourth, training schedules and systems are definitized. Successful managers do not leave training to chance or hope. They spell out what the agency has to offer in this area and then they deliver.

In the more sophisticated agency, as has already been mentioned, the emphasis will be placed on advanced subjects. Outside experts in various fields will serve as guest instructors or lecturers. Chartered Life Underwriter courses including the advanced degree work will be promoted as well as attendance at CLU institutes. In keeping with the management style in the agency, the future thrust of the training program will be to prepare all associates to sell successfully and profitably in the upper income markets, including business insurance and estate planning. Financial planning will be their marketing strategy utilizing the full gamut of products including all forms of tax shelters, equities, etc., as well as traditional life products.

In the more traditional agency the emphasis on training will be no less structured and organized. Considerable emphasis will be on skill-building sessions using audiovisual for role-playing sessions. Considerable emphasis will be placed on fully understanding the whole life contract and the many ways it can be presented to make it attractive to the buying public. Computer prepared illustrations will be included at no cost or low cost from the home office or agency. Basic training programs may be administered in groups with some additional sessions on the basics of business insurance and simple estate planning. An understanding of the general needs for insurance will be developed, including in many instances the need for multiline coverages—auto, home owners, health, disability and small group. The overall emphasis will be on the importance of developing large numbers of clients for whom the agent can handle all or most of his or her insurance needs. Teaching the agent to prospect for this type of potential client will have high priority. LUTC parts I and II will be required for each new agent.

As indicated above, each major city has many agencies who fit one or the other of these descriptions with certain variations. But all of them are by no means doing well. The successful manager does not kid himself or anyone else. He understands his style. He knows the knowledge and skills his associates must acquire for them to penetrate the market his company expects him to serve. He concentrates on the delivery of that program and the follow-through with each associate—and that is another reason he is successful.

E. Planning

Fifth, planning is an integral part of the success in each type of agency. Many excellent articles have been written on this subject. LIMRA's Agency Management Training Course devotes several sessions to planning and they are excellent. In Bill Wallace's book, *Doing Better,* he covers this subject superbly and if you haven't read it and studied it you should.

It is probably safe to say that just about all managers and general agents plan. Most home offices, if not all, demand that something in the way of a "plan" be sent to them at year-end as a guide to establishing company production goals. My experience, however, is that most of these plans concern themselves for the most part with "how much." The agency vice president has to come up with a total and he needs the imput of each agency head to help him develop reasonable figures.

The successful manager does not stop with "how much." In fact, that is generally the result *of the planning process.* The most important part of planning to these successful managers is the answering of four questions—what, how, who, when. Developing answers for these questions for every aspect of the agency operation at an in-depth planning session with the supervisory staff *away from the office* is the secret to a sound overall agency plan—including how much. And that is exactly what successful managers do.

Short-range plans—up to one year—will be the main emphasis of these planning sessions. Successful managers have a pretty good general concept of what their long-range goals are. But they know that their success will be determined by establishing a day-by-day, week-by-week, month-by-month agency plan which can be effectively administered and which will serve as a basis for keeping the agency on track. Successful managers do an excellent job of planning, but maybe even more important is the follow-through they give in making certain everyone is involved with the plan and its effective administration during the entire year.

F. Business Decisions

Sixth, they work hard developing their capacity to exercise good judgment in the making of business decisions. General agents and managers can lose their jobs and go broke by making bad decisions, particularly those directly involved with money. To be successful a manager must have good judgment—and exercise it—and a solid decision-making style can be developed. This subject is discussed at some length in the chapter on agency leadership (Chapter 3). However, here are six methods I have used to help me improve my percentage of good decisions:

1. Take your time. Rarely is a quick decision necessary.
2. Use the balance sheet. Reduce positive and negative points to writing. Not new but effective.
3. Never mail a "questionable" letter the day you write it. Sleep on it at least, and you may decide not to mail it after all.
4. Concentrate on becoming a good listener. Get *all* the facts and think about them before you decide on a course of action. Your judgment can never be any better than your facts.
5. Do not establish precedents that you cannot live with —service, physical quarters, financial, etc.
6. Do not promise more than you can deliver. If you once lose credibility, it is difficult if not impossible ever to get it back!

Management style certainly is not limited to these areas but they are key points and they do play a highly significant role in helping a manager or general agent achieve success.

Before leaving management style I would like to quote from the March 11, 1974 issue of *Sports Illustrated.* As sports fans will recall, Walter Alston managed the Los Angeles Dodgers baseball team for 23-plus years, always with a one-year contract. His managerial record was one of the most successful in major league baseball history.

Let me quote directly from the magazine:

> Originally Alston was hired because it was felt his approach was right for a particular group of play-

> ers. That belief, vindicated by the 1955 World Series victory, has grown into a conviction, widely held, that *Alston's style* would contribute to the success of *any* team. The brilliant and often temperamental minds of the Durochers and the Martins produce no more victories than do the less brilliant but still adequate minds of men like Alston. Certainly one needs a modicum of baseball knowledge to manage well, but an excess produces no additional return. Brilliance, with its capricious outbursts, is often a burden to the front office and disruptive to a team's composure; witness Martin's problems with the Yankees. Alston's modest and unassuming nature tends to diffuse tensions. Indeed, there is no locker room in baseball more placid than that of the Los Angeles Dodgers. Alston's tendency is to let an event evolve to its natural conclusion without his interference.

I would suggest that there just might be a moral for all of us in management as we read about the "management style" of one of baseball's all-time most successful managers.

2. CAPITALIZING ON STRENGTHS

Another reason why general agents and managers succeed is that they learn to **capitalize on their strengths and somehow compensate for their weaknesses.**

There are many major responsibilities in the management of a successful agency. No one person can be equally strong in all areas. Furthermore, there may be certain aspects of the job that the manager enjoys doing far more than other parts. And in a large agency there is simply so much to be done that a substantial staff may be an absolute necessity. What is the answer? Attract and develop associates for specialized responsibilities that the manager either does not do well, does not like to do, or does not have time to do. However, for this approach to function effectively, the manager must, in fact, delegate the responsibility and permit the associate to perform and grow on his own.

Another quote from the *Sports Illustrated* article on Walt Alston illustrates the point.

> Over the years Alston has become known as an expert at delegating authority to his coaches. One L.A. pitcher says, "If we tell the pitching coach we don't want to run on a certain day, he doesn't have to check with Walt to see if it is OK. He makes his own decision."

The successful agency manager is a Walt Alston type of delegater. He knows he cannot do it all. If he intends to build a large sophisticated agency he will need in-office technicians in various products and systems to back up the sales force. He will also need knowledgeable supervisors to work with new and established agents in the field—demonstrating and closing large cases in the advanced markets. Of course, someone will have to be responsible for adding new people. No agency ever survived over a period of time without quality recruiting. Obviously he cannot do it all. So he brings into the organization associates to whom he can assign certain of these responsibilities. And then he gives them considerable freedom to perform on their own. At regular intervals there will be progress reports so that the manager can be certain the operation is proceeding according to plan. However, the day-by-day decisions will be made by the individual to whom the responsibility has been assigned.

The same situation applies in the more traditional agency and all variations thereof. The successful manager attracts and trains associates to do the things he doesn't do well or doesn't like to do. For example, let's assume the manager enjoys recruiting and working with agents and supervisors "one-on-one," setting goals, building confidence, increasing expectation levels, etc., and he is very good in all these areas.

If he concentrates on performing to his maximum in these highly important activities and delegates for the most part the day-by-day training, technical knowledge and field supervision to competent associates, he has the nucleus of a highly successful agency. Of course, he must have a reporting system which will keep him informed of what is happening. And he must be prepared to take remedial action without too much delay when the situation calls for it.

There are many possibilities as to how agency functions can be assigned. However, the manager always has the ultimate responsibility. He either must do it himself or he must see to it that someone else does it. It is as simple as that. But the successful manager recognizes his limitations and his strengths and he develops a management staff that *collectively* performs the functions required to build a successful agency for the company he represents.

3. BELIEF IN A LIFE INSURANCE CAREER

The third reason general agents and managers succeed is their **abiding belief in the worthwhileness and importance of a career in life insurance—particularly the career agents' job— plus a deep personal loyalty to the company they represent.** It is this belief that makes them great recruiters. They are convinced they represent a great company and that they have an exceptional opportunity for the right candidate. They speak with conviction and sincerity which makes what they say highly convincing to a prospective recruit. They strive to provide for their associates the best office space, back-up assistance, etc., that they can get the company to pay for. If the company won't provide it and they feel it is important, they dig down in their pockets and pay for it themselves. They appreciate the overriding importance of the sales force to the success of the enterprise and they go out of their way to show them appreciation at every legitimate opportunity.

The manager who is not truly sold on the career aspects of selling life insurance will never be a successful manager.

Let me give you an example. Some 25 years ago I had a casual conversation with the general agent of another company. He was an attractive, intelligent gentleman of about my age. I was favorably impressed with him until he said, "Lew, I don't think there is a future in this business for a career agent, do you?" I replied in the affirmative and quickly terminated the conversation. I did not want to listen to any negative thinking about the future of the agent then or now. It is interesting but not surprising to note that not too long after our conversation this particular individual was relieved as general agent. Later he found an industry job and would you believe he is now a high level officer with a company that gives lip service to building an agency force while it actively solicits brokerage business. I wonder how he feels about the future of the agency system today.

The manager has a responsibility to help every associate develop to the maximum of his potential. He sets the example and creates the proper atmosphere because of his conviction and that is part of the reason he is successful.

It is my experience that invariably when a manager starts "bad mouthing" his company he is on his way out. However, if a high percentage of the leading managers of a particular company are unhappy at the same time, which sometimes happens, the agency officers would be well advised to get to the bottom of the problem and see what can be done to improve the situation as quickly as possible.

The successful manager demonstrates pride in his company at every reasonable opportunity—to present associates, agents and clerical staff, to the public whenever he meets with groups of people and, of course, to policyholders who appreciate being reassured they selected the right company for their insurance coverage. Although they will not hesitate to make constructive, well thought out suggestions to the home office, I have never known a *successful manager or general agent* who wasn't a real booster for his company.

4. CAPACITY TO ADJUST TO CHANGE

The fourth reason general agents and managers succeed is that **they have the capacity to adjust to company changes in goals and policy, industry changes, product revolutions, economic ups and downs, etc.**

Someone once said, "He who fights the future has a dangerous enemy." I believe that the managers who don't accept change readily in the future will be wasting a great deal of time fighting when they would be better off concentrating on adjusting. Companies have varying marketing objectives. There was a time when the easiest way for a manager to determine what his company's goals were was to study his compensation system. But that isn't necessarily true anymore. Changes in the marketplace and the proliferation of new products happen so frequently that many times the compensation system cannot be changed quickly enough to recognize and promote the company's goals. But over the long period it is probably still the best overall guide to what the company wants the manager to do in his agency. Certainly, when the company discovers it is not serving that function, contract changes to make the necessary correction will be effected immediately.

Currently changes are taking place almost constantly in three areas. One is individual company changes. You know what your company has done in recent months but undoubtedly there are more changes coming. There really isn't any way you control what will happen so all you can do is prepare yourself and your agency to adjust. Better still you can recognize that you are part of an exciting period—expect changes, welcome them, adapt to them, and go on to bigger things. That is what the successful managers will do.

Another is product changes and other industry changes. They will continue and perhaps accelerate. There is no point in discussing the pros and cons of the current status because it is a "moving target" and no one knows when, where or if it will end. However, there are two points successful managers keep everlastingly in mind—people buy life insurance primarily because somebody loves somebody. They always have and there is every reason to have confidence they always will. Those qualities and abilities that enabled successful managers to enjoy above average incomes in the past will enable them to do very well in the future. But it may require some adjusting and this they must be prepared to do.

There is a third type of change that the manager must cope with—economic ups and downs. However, successful managers know that they have little, if any, effect on our business if the manager maintains the right attitude and provides positive leadership. I know this from personal experience. In 1970, Seattle had 20% unemployment (Boeing cutback). A billboard near the airport read, "Will the last person to leave Seattle please turn out the lights?" To say the least, it was not the "best of times." However, the Seattle Agency of Prudential, of which I was then the manager, produced in excess of $1,000,000 of new net premiums, the first agency in the history of the company to do so. That isn't much of a production record today but back in 1970 it was quite impressive in Prudential.

Yes, I am convinced that our business can always be good. Unemployment and replacement may increase lapse rates and cause agents to prospect more selectively—but it makes available more outstanding potential recruits. Successful managers are aware of this and they will always do well.

I have discussed four basic reasons why managers succeed:

- They develop their individual management style—and they follow it consistently and persistently. They do not try to be like someone else.
- They learn to capitalize on their strengths and somehow compensate for individual weaknesses—they

figure out a way to find people to do what they do not do well, do not like to do or do not have time to do.

- They have an abiding belief in the worthwhileness of life insurance and the career agent's job.

- They have developed the capacity to adjust to the inevitable changes in company goals and policy, industry changes and economic ups and downs.

They are all important—and you have heard them all discussed before. But probably you have read and heard less on the importance of being able to adjust than any of the others. Here are some serious thoughts on that subject.

It seems to me that the insurance business, and life itself for that matter, involves a constant series of adjustments. As children, our first major adjustment starts on our first day at school. Junior high calls for another adjustment and high school for most boys and girls was and is a major adjustment. Our first part-time job and certainly our first full-time job requires us to develop rather quickly a different perspective. When we first leave home, either to attend college, enter the military service or to move out of the environment in which we grew up, and support ourselves, it is a big change.

Then, we marry—and what an adjustment that is for most of us! Many people simply cannot cope with this situation for various reasons and too high a percentage of marriages end in divorce—which calls for a special adjustment. The next challenge for most people occurs when the first child comes. Further adjustments are necessary as other children arrive. And now we have the entire cycle being repeated—the children facing their individual adjustments and the parents a new situation as the children grow up and leave home. A further critical adjustment is necessary when the couple is left alone—just the two of them—with the kids gone and on their own. Next we have the retirement years and this requires considerable planning if a successful transition is to be made.

And then the final adjustment comes when one of the two passes away and the survivor is left alone.

The final point I would like to make is this: You and I have been faced with a constant stream of situations which have required us to adjust and we will be faced with such situations as long as we live. As we have discussed, they occur in both our business lives and our personal lives. The capacity to adjust, it seems to me, has never been more important than it is currently. Our ability to make adjustments has been and is the secret to whatever happiness and success we have found. For the need to adjust is a fact of life.

* * *

3.

AGENCY LEADERSHIP

A great number of articles have been written and many speeches delivered on the subject of leadership. One of the finest appeared in a publication with an original copyright of 1947. The booklet is entitled "Human Relations in Management" and the concluding chapter is a discussion of leadership. It is well worth reading.

Later on I will quote from that booklet. However, I want to mention it at the outset to make the point that very little new or different has been written or said on this subject since 1947 and probably well before that. The difficulty we all have is remembering and practicing what we know. Leadership ability is a skill and as such can diminish or even be lost if we do not work at it constantly.

If you wish to purchase copies of the booklet, contact:

LIMRA
Box 208
Hartford, CT 06141

My purpose in this chapter is to refresh your memory and at the same time share with you some of the convictions and techniques I have personally found useful in discharging the responsibilities of an agency head.

THE "LENGTHENED SHADOW" CONCEPT

It has been said, and I believe properly so, that an agency is the "lengthened shadow" of the manager or general agent. In other words, the best way to lead an agency in the direction one would have it go is by example. Our associates are much more impressed by what we do than they are by what we say.

For example, if the manager wants his associates to become Chartered Life Underwriters it is imperative that he set the example by personally earning the designation. If he wants them to pursue CLU work and later become Chartered Financial Consultants, the manager must again lead the way.

Furthermore, the most effective way to involve his associates in LUTC classes is first to moderate a class himself, and later have some of his senior associates serve as moderators on an ongoing basis. If this is done, CLU and LUTC study becomes the accepted standard and it is relatively easy to have a high degree of participation.

The same technique of personal example can also be employed in promoting activity in other groups such as industry associations, religious denominations, service clubs and other civic groups. It can also be used to encourage a healthier life style including the need for regular exercise.

In all of these areas, and others too numerous to mention, the manager's example has a profound impact—much more than most managers understand and accept.

The importance of setting a good example is by no means a new concept. But, like other basics of successful agency management, it is too often ignored. The result may not be catastrophic, but the progress of the agency may not be satisfactory to the agency—or the home office. Furthermore, there is a possibility no one will perceive that it is the manager's failure to lead by example which is the root of the problem. It does not stand out like poor recruiting and retention results or financial mismanagement.

ATTITUDES—GOOD AND BAD

Quite often this leadership weakness shows up in the manager's attitude. I am familiar with agencies in which the general opinion is that the home office rarely does anything right; underwriting is slow and too conservative; business conditions are terrible; and, of course, recruiting is very difficult if not impossible for many reasons including all of the above. A few minutes of conversation with the manager will reveal that it is his negative attitude which has created this climate. It is unlikely that a successful agency will ever be developed under these conditions.

Undoubtedly, there are instances where there is validity to some or even all of these complaints. However, it is bad judgment to discuss them in the agency. It can only be counterproductive. Certainly efforts should be made to effect changes at the home office in those areas where the manager has strong feelings. It is my experience that home office executives are receptive to well documented complaints. The key words are *well documented.* It makes no sense to complain in generalities. It is a waste of time and effort.

The manager should always recognize that his attitude is contagious. If he expects his associates to have a positive attitude and good morale, he must be everlastingly conscious of the example he sets.

The manager should always radiate confidence—always be optimistic even though he may have just lost his leading agent! This is when he needs the *conviction* that he can *recruit* beyond every problem—past, present and future. And, if he really believes this, he can! He should always remember that insecurity and lack of self-confidence are also contagious and are sensed by others. It is imperative that the manager conceal his own troubles and be cheerful in spite of difficulties. No matter how upset his personal life may be, he should never discuss his problems with agency associates. This isn't easy to avoid doing. All of us need someone on whom to "dump our load."

One answer is a patient and understanding spouse. However, if this solution is not available or is inadequate, fellow managers in one's own company, manager competitors, home office vice presidents and directors of agencies are possibilities. Visiting with professionals—ministers, priests, rabbis—can be very helpful. And there may be occasions when spending some time with an understanding physician or even a psychiatrist or psychologist should be considered.

Some managers like to appear important by denigrating home office people. This is the poorest form of leadership. We need each other. Home office people are human too. They respond to appreciation and goodwill and it is good leadership to treat them with respect and dignity. I have also known a few managers who went out of their way to belittle other companies and/or other distribution systems and sometimes other professionals such as lawyers. This is self-defeating. It is impossible to build up one's own organization by tearing down other organizations and/or other people. It won't work and those who try to do so are merely demonstrating their own insecurity.

REWARDS OF RELIABILITY

The good leader is honest, sincere and reliable. He does what he says he will do and never promises more than he can deliver. As an example, this is particularly important in his relations with established agents. He should have clear-cut, well-publicized criteria for determining office space and secretarial assistance. These are critical areas to an agent and the manager must honor them or he loses all credibility as a leader.

The good leader does not exaggerate what he has done or what he has to offer, especially when he is interviewing prospective associates. If a new associate discovers he has been misled, he will never completely trust the one who misled him. It was suggested to me when I came into the business that I conduct all interviews as if my agency vice president were sitting on one side of me and the state insurance commissioner on the other side. I still think that is good advice and I recommend it.

It is important that the leader conduct himself in such a way that people who meet him for the first time instinctively feel that they can trust him. Being an empathetic listener tends to win confidence which in turn builds trust. The leader should guard against doing or saying anything that will in any way diminish this initial feeling of trust.

The good leader tries his best to be the same sort of person every day so that his associates feel they know him. It adds to their security. A manager with many changes of mood is never fully understood or trusted. It is unfortunate if people wonder "what mood the old man is in today." It isn't easy to reflect a consistent aura of confidence and dependability. But that is the challenge of leadership.

EXERCISING SOUND JUDGMENT

If there is one ability that is absolutely essential to lead a successful agency, it is the capacity to exercise sound judgment. Through the years I have observed agency heads adopt courses of action with minimal chances to be successful.

An example comes to mind immediately: spending money opening detached offices without strong and capable supervisors to manage them. Quite often this is done when the time and money could be spent far more intelligently (and profitably) in the agency office.

I once heard a speaker observe that if you want to build character in a person you must "start with his grandmother." Although obviously a tongue in cheek statement, heredity does play a part both in character and judgment. However, four simple rules have helped me. Perhaps they will help you.

1. Never make a quick decision unless absolutely forced to do so by circumstances. (Rarely does this happen.)

2. Always consider all the other options before acting.

3. Have discussions with and ask for opinions from people whose judgment you respect.

4. Reduce the pros and cons to writing before making any decision that you consider reasonably important and particularly if it involves the lives of other people, as it generally does.

MAINTAINING A BALANCE

Ours is a volatile business. There are high moments—when everything seems to be going great. And there are other times when it seems that everything is going wrong. In order to maintain the proper balance in approaching the decision-making process, it is important to recognize that, no matter how well things seem to be going, they are not quite as good as they seem. And by the same token, when they seem bad they really aren't quite as bad as they seem. If we accept this, we can avoid those high peaks and low valleys which are so frustrating and on occasion can lead us to make an emotional decision which we may regret later.

Oftentimes the typical manager of a mediocre or failing agency considers himself to be the boss. He wants his associates to be his puppets and he wants to pull the strings. On the other hand, the manager of the outstanding agency is a leader instead of a boss. And there is a distinct difference. A number of years ago, LIMRA did a study which developed the following very interesting points.

- The boss drives his associates; the leader coaches them.
- The boss depends on authority; the leader on goodwill.
- The boss inspires fear; the leader inspires enthusiasm.
- The boss says "I"; the leader says "We."
- The boss makes work a drudgery; the leader makes it a game.
- The boss says "Go"; the leader says "Let's go."

COMMUNICATIONS

Good communications are absolutely essential for the agency leader to be effective. However, they just don't happen—they have to be worked at. If the leader makes himself available whenever his associates want to see him and if he is sincerely interested in their point of view, he has made a good start. He should make certain that he has personal contact with each member of the organization on a regular basis. In some instances it may have to be by telephone and many times it may only be for a few minutes. But it is important that the contact be made so that each individual knows the manager is interested in him or her as a person.

There are times when the leader is placed in the position of having to change the point of view of one of his associates on some subject. However, before he tries to "make the sale" he should listen first to what his associate has to say. It has been said that "people only hear the answers to questions they have asked." It is difficult to make quick changes in an associate's behavior. However, if the manager maintains good communications they can be helped to change themselves.

I subscribe to what I call the "refrigerator theory." The only way one person can move a refrigerator is to "walk it" —twist it one way and then the other. It cannot be grabbed and pushed or pulled very successfully. The same approach can often be used in changing the point of view or behavior of our associates. We can move them a little bit in one direction and then a little bit in another direction and, if we persist, we can achieve considerable success in having them accept our suggestions and making the progress we would like to have them make.

Let us consider a specific example of how this theory might work. Perhaps you have one or more associates whom you would like to have write more of their business in the advanced markets. It has been my experience that it is unlikely this will happen until the individual is comfortable working with prospects who earn substantial incomes and enjoy a relatively high degree of success in their chosen fields.

The first requirement for this to happen is for the agent to acquire the necessary knowledge which is readily available from many sources including American College, Advanced LUTC course, etc. It has been my experience that it is much easier to sell the agent on acquiring the knowledge than it is to get him or her to take it into the field and use it. The problem is that even armed with adequate knowledge the agent still does not feel comfortable dealing with people whom he perceives as being "out of his class." Also, he lacks confidence that he is capable of successfully completing the total sales process with this type of prospect. These are two separate problems and must be approached individually.

First, you might consider getting the agent involved in his local life underwriters association. As an active member and later as an officer he or she will be recognized as a professional by his peers which will improve his self-image and make him more comfortable dealing with other successful people. Encouraging activity in service clubs can also serve the same purpose and at the same time enable him to associate with successful people from other fields in a nonthreatening atmosphere.

Encouraging associates to join country clubs, athletic clubs, tennis clubs, etc., and become active in them is another way for an agent to become comfortable being with people who make and have money. In a short time he or she will realize that there really aren't any basic differences in people, no matter how successful they are, and in many respects the more successful they are the easier it is to do business with them.

But even after the agent is feeling much more comfortable in social situations with higher income prospects, and even though he does have a good depth of knowledge in the advanced markets, he still may lack confidence that he is capable of completing the sale process with this type of prospect. At this point in the agent's career you might want to sell him on working jointly with a senior agent who has a track record of closing business in the advanced markets. After a few cases in which the junior agent for the most part is an observer, in all likelihood he will conclude that he can do it himself and make 100% of the commission. When this happens he is on his way.

This step-by-step process will work in many situations. It is the best method I know to effect this kind of behavioral change—and it just may be the only way. People do not change old habits readily. But they will change if we work with them thoughtfully and intelligently. The "refrigerator theory" has helped me in doing this successfully.

There is no doubt that the leader's expectations are the key to an associate's performance and development. This is commonly referred to as "Pygmalion in management" in reference to the sculptor in Greek mythology who carved a statue of a beautiful woman who subsequently was brought to life. If the manager consistently expects more and more from his associates, he will inevitably see it come about.

There are many opportunities to do this. One, of course, is in the Annual Planning Session. Here the manager has an opportunity to upgrade the associate's thinking regarding the life style he or she might like to become accustomed to. The need for extra income becomes apparent and increased production the solution. The manager should encourage the associate to think bigger and at the same time assure him or her that he is confident the associate is capable of *far more* than he has ever done. Consisent reassurance that he is capable of achieving the higher level, whatever it may be, will quite often result in its attainment.

The same strategy can be used in establishing goals for sales campaigns. It is relatively easy to gradually raise the production requirements in order to receive whatever recognition is being offered. If this is done on a consistent basis, the results of all associates will gradually increase to the point that they are achieving much higher production than they would have conceived possible earlier in their careers. A similar approach can be used in establishing production requirements for office space and secretarial allowances. And, of course, promotion of the National Sales Achievement Award, Million Dollar Round Table and Top of the Table can also be effective.

The manager should consistently strive to convince his associates that they are better than they think they are. If he works at it consistently and intelligently they will in fact become better and better.

RECOGNITION

The good leader does not hesitate to give recognition to his associates. In fact, he should welcome the opportunity and recognize their accomplishments at every valid opportunity. However, the recognition must be sincere. "Phony" compliments are worse than none at all. They should recognize special performance at a definite time. Well-earned recognition given in front of one's peers and/or family is like "nectar from the gods." None of us ever gets enough of that wonderful stuff.

A well-known industry executive and a long-time personal friend told me a true story which demonstrates the point. At the time the incident occurred the executive was a general agent. One of his outstanding agents had played a relatively modest role at the local life underwriters association luncheon meeting. But he had performed very well and the general agent was proud of him.

When they returned to the agency he asked the agent into his office and complimented him on how well he had discharged his assignment at the meeting. Knowing that this particular individual enjoyed being recognized as much or more than most of us, he was quite profuse in his compliments. Just before they formally broke up, however, the agent's secretary came in and said he was wanted on the telephone. Some 30 minutes later the agent came back to the general agent's office and said "Now, ________, where were you?"

This actual experience demonstrates a number of key points in the leadership process. First, the general agent was sincere. He believed the agent had done a good job. Second, the recognition was for specific performance at a specific time and it was immediate. Delayed recognition tends to make the receiver question its sincerity. It may come across somewhat as an afterthought. And third, it demonstrates that in his particular instance the individual had an almost insatiable need for recognition from his general agent.

Personal recognition from our superiors means a great deal to all of us if we are totally honest with ourselves. The good leader never forgets this and he takes advantage of every opportunity to give sincere recognition to his associates. Production accomplishments are generally recognized and they have their place. Oftentimes, however, the personal touch I have described above can mean more than being recognized as a top producer.

As I have indicated above, I am a great believer in using industry associations and training facilities to help associates grow. For example, during the 30 years I managed the Seattle Agency for Prudential, the presidencies of *22* industry organizations (LUA, GAMA, CLU) were served by members of our agency! As the fellow says, "That may not be a record but it has to be a darn good average," and I am proud of this contribution they have made. I am sure this activity has been influenced by the example I have tried to set in my own association activities and I am convinced it was a substantial growth experience for many of the individuals involved.

Furthermore, I believe it is good agency leadership to promote LUTC, CLU and MDRT on a consistent basis. These organizations make a tremendous contribution to the industry and it is simply good judgment for the agency manager to have his people involved. Managing an agency is not an easy job and the leader should use all the assistance that is available to him, particularly when it is as helpful as these organizations can be.

LOYALTY

I have already pointed out how important a part the manager's example plays in the process of an agency, both by the individual members and the organization as a whole. There is another important area where the manager's example is all important. I am referring to the key quality of loyalty. If the manager is not 100% loyal to his company he certainly should not be surprised if his associates tend to be disloyal. Furthermore, if the manager's loyalty to his associates leaves something to be desired—if he regularly tends to put his own interests ahead of theirs—he cannot expect much loyalty in return.

I recognize that it is possible for a manager to be too loyal—particularly to those associates who don't deserve his loyalty for any one of a number of reasons. There are occasions when a more realistic course of action might be to terminate the relationship without delay. However, I believe in the long run an agency will have better morale and achieve greater results in an environment where loyalty as demonstrated by the manager is a way of life.

CONCENTRATING ON FUNDAMENTALS

There are no simple answers which will provide the secrets to successful agency leadership. The answer lies in concentrating on the fundamentals. The LIMRA publication mentioned at the start of this chapter says it so well:

> Many people talk about leaders being born. Leaders as such are not born, they are made; they make themselves. The reason people think leaders are born is that some people develop within themselves the *habits* of leadership—the *habits* of setting a good example, of giving ego-recognition, of building a sense of security, etc. These habits, then, become so deeply ingrained in such a person that they are done naturally—they are a part of a habit stream, and a person does a good job of leadership not because he or she was born that way but more because he or she is governed by leadership habits.

THE MATTER OF EGO

There is another factor, however, which cannot be ignored. It is the matter of ego. All people involved in life insurance sales must have strong egos—almost indestructible ones. There are so many turndowns, so many possible disappointments, that a fragile ego would turn a person out of the business in a matter of months.

But a strong ego, unless harnessed, can cause its owner a lot of grief. It must consciously be kept in check at all times. This is particularly true of the manager, who must coddle the egos of his people without exhibiting his own unduly.

Ego is the characteristic which will keep an agency manager or an agent driving hard long after he has earned enough money to satisfy his family needs regularly. Robert Browning put it subtly when he wrote, "A man's reach must exceed his grasp, or what's a heaven for?" But an overblown ego, which can be acquired by too much praise from subordinates in the field or executives in the home office, can be destructible. It can cause its owner to reach too far, possibly without the qualifications necessary for success.

In my own case, one of the greatest tests of keeping my ego in balance was the year *after* I had been president of the National Association of Life Underwriters. For 12 months I had traveled extensively, lived in the presidential suites at the best hotels, been the key speaker at national meetings of some consequence, and acquired all the trappings of a chief executive. Then, one day in September, a door closed and the applause stopped. I was now a past president, one of many. And when the cameras clicked, they weren't taking *my* picture.

No more standing ovations, no more easy praise—which had come to me because of my position. From that point forward, I had to *earn* it all again. I realized the fact quickly, and undertook to adjust as rapidly as possible. I believe I made the adjustment; if I hadn't, it would have been difficult to return to the comparatively small confines of my agency. If I had felt that all the pleasant tumult of the past year had been because of *me,* rather than my position, I probably wouldn't be living the happy life that had been my lot.

Andy Warhol, who is an observer of the New York scene, has said, "All of us are likely to be famous for about 15 minutes." That's certainly true of us in the life insurance field: a pleasant run of success in our agency, a massive case we are able to crack, election to a position that sets us above our colleagues for a moment, and so on. If we cannot return to earth after having been in that brief stratosphere, we will be hurt—sometimes irreparably.

The manager should examine his or her ego constantly: Am I letting it show too much? Am I letting my reputation affect my judgment? Do I give the appearance of looking down on many of my colleagues? If any of these things—and many others which will come easily to the reader's mind—seems true, then a change of course is in order.

I don't believe anyone has all the answers to effective agency leadership. However, by concentrating on the fundamentals which we have been discussing the results will come.

The philosopher, William James, said it so well: "Let no youth have any anxiety about the upshot of his education, whatever the line of it may be. If he keeps faithfully busy each hour of the working day, he may safely leave the final results to itself. He can with perfect certainty count on waking up *some fine morning* to find himself one of the competent ones of his generation, in whatever pursuit he may have singled out. Silently between all the details of his business, the power of judgment in all that *class of matter* will have built itself up within him as a possession that will never pass."

DEVELOPING LEADERSHIP ABILITY

Leadership ability can be developed. It is a skill that can be learned. Leaders are not just born. For most of us it is simply a matter of self-discipline—the same thing managers are always talking about to their agents. We know what to do, we simply do not do it as consistently and persistently as we should. We form bad habits both in our personal and our business lives. And we make poor decisions. There is an old legend about a skylark that illustrates the story very well:

"It seems that a skylark was about to soar into the heavens to sing her morning song when she noticed an old man passing by with a basket of worms. The skylark offered to exchange one of the feathers for a worm. The old man consented. The same thing happened the next morning and the next. And then it happened morning after morning. From day to day there was only a slight change in the skylark's looks or ability to fly. However, her flight gradually became less swift and on a lowering level. Finally a morning came when she was unable to lift herself into the sky. Only when she was grounded did she realize that she had exchanged too many feathers for worms.

"Then she decided to buy her feathers back. She spent many days digging for worms and finally she went to the old man and said, 'I would like to give you this basket full of worms and get back my feathers.'

" 'Not so,' said the tradesman, 'My business is worms for feathers, not feathers for worms.' "

All leaders are constantly challenged to make decisions and value judgments. Most are relatively minor but some are of major importance to the organization; the decisions they make and the example they set can have a profound affect on the lives of countless people. The moral in that old legend is profound and the agency head would be well advised to heed the lesson it teaches.

This is particularly true as he evaluates the agency recruiting procedures and selection standards. My mother often quoted the old saw, "You cannot make a silk purse out of a sow's ear." And she was so right! To build a quality organization, a leader needs quality people and for the agency head it starts with the type of new associates placed under contract.

Taking shortcuts in the agency training and supervisory programs, tolerating corner cutting in the sales process and sloppy service to policyholders are additional examples of "trading feathers for worms." Sooner or later a price will be paid for this type of leadership, just as the skylark did, and the agency will never achieve the success the manager so greatly desires.

It is important to accept that leadership cannot be bought or transferred. Furthermore, having a title does not make a leader. The challenge to all of us who have been placed in leadership positions is to earn the right to lead by our day-by-day conduct. It is a rewarding opportunity and well worth our total commitment.

* * *

4.

THE M'S OF MANAGEMENT

It has been my experience that success in any management tends to come to a general agent or manager in direct relation to his ability to understand and master certain basic concepts and activities. In this chapter I will explore four such areas—manpower, morale, momentum and motivation.

Much of this material was presented by me from the platform at the March 1969 LAMP Meeting of the General Agents and Managers Conference. However, in reviewing it I believe these four points are just as pertinent as they were then, despite all the changes that have taken place in the industry during the past 15 years.

(In this section particularly—although it pertains everywhere—I ask the reader when I use the term "manpower" or "man" or "he," that the feminine equivalent be taken for granted. I find it tedious both to write and read something that tries to bow to both sexes in every sentence. As women become more prominent in all areas of life insurance, almost all masculine nouns and pronouns should be read as though they referred to both sexes.)

M #1 — MANPOWER

The first "M" of management is manpower. To be even more specific let's call it the *development* of manpower. This is the first M of management by any standard one cares to use. It always has been and it always will be. Coy Eklund, former chairman of the board of the Equitable Society and at one time the manager of a large Equitable agency, once made the following statement which I feel is most profound. Coy said:

> The objective of agency management must be recognized as being foremost the development of manpower (womanpower). That is what the job requires. It's not the requirement of the company, the agency vice president or the director of agencies. It's just what the job requires. It's what staying in business requires.

The manager needs to realize that in the final analysis no one will find and build people for him. Managers have to do it for themselves. Have you ever thought or said (or heard some other manager make the statement), "All I need is a couple of good supervisors and I could really move out"? I have heard certain agency heads whom I know personally make that statement over a period of *several years*—and they are still making it! In other words, they have been aware of their need for additional people, in various categories including supervisory help, but they have not developed it. Apparently they are expecting someone else to do it for them and this rarely happens on a sound permanent basis.

It is possible, I suppose, to proselyte supervisory help from other companies. Personally, I am not in favor of this approach and I never did it. It has been my observation that too often it doesn't work out. Chances are he won't be any more loyal to his new manager than he was to the one he left and, in my opinion, if there is one quality that is most important in a supervisor it is loyalty. The way to have loyal supervisors is to bring them in as agents and have them develop in your own agency. This can be done if the manager recognizes its importance and gives it high priority among his agency goals. Obviously he needs to recruit on a regular basis a goodly number of new agents whose age, education and background characteristics are such that they are potential supervisors. If this is done on a consistent basis, some of them will be (or can be) interested in supervisory work. As a result the manager will always be in a position to appoint a new supervisor from his own organization whenever the need arises.

Let us consider two agencies, both of which need a supervisor right now. One manager decides to hire one from another company and after several attempts over a period of several months is finally successful. Keep in mind that this individual is totally unfamiliar with his new company's training program, selling system, products, agency philosophy, financing plan, etc. Furthermore, the manager knows very little about him and his abilities. There is a good chance that in about two and a half or three years a mutual decision will be made that it has not worked out and the manager again will be looking for a supervisor.

The other manager, as part of his agency philosophy, decides to "grow his own." He recruits "management trainees" on a consistent basis. In two years or maybe even less, if he gives this activity sufficient priority, he will have the supervisor he needs. But what a difference! This manager has a supervisor who is familiar with the company and the agency. He knows the products and the agent financing plan for he probably has been on it. The manager knows the individual and his abilities from two years of working with him or her. Not only are the odds in favor of his being successful, but also if the manager is "working the system," he will have a pool of potential supervisors on an ongoing basis.

I think it is desirable to distinguish between the "development of men (or women)" and the "development of manpower." Granted that this cannot be done completely. I believe there are important differences.

For example, there tends to be an emotional involvement when one thinks of developing individual people. When the approach is to develop "manpower" the approach is far more objective, which I feel is necessary. To illustrate—the successful surgeon performs many operations. He gives to each the best of his professional ability. But not all of his operations are successful. Some of his patients die. But he cannot permit himself to become emotionally involved with his patients or he would find it difficult to survive the constant personal trauma to which he would be exposed.

As agency heads we must take the same approach for our own mental and emotional health. We should do the best we can with each new recruit, but not become emotionally involved when they fail—as unfortunately many of them will. Hugh Bell, outstanding general agent with the Equitable of Iowa in Seattle many years ago and my personal mentor, once confided to me, "I have difficulty remembering a failure's name when I meet him on the street just a few weeks after he terminates." I think Hugh was on the right track and for our own peace of mind we need to develop a similar philosophy.

When we are trying to develop *individuals* or help them survive, we tend to stay too long with people destined ultimately for failure or mediocrity. And I have done my share of that. When we think *manpower* we terminate early and hire somebody else. We all know that slow starters seldom succeed. All the studies prove this conclusively. So why should we try to beat the odds?

When the manager's prime objective is the "development of men," he tends to put his or her eggs into too few baskets. As a result the agency head becomes extremely vulnerable to unexpected and unforeseen turnover. If, instead, he is concentrating on the development of "manpower," there is more of a tendency to "spread the risk" with greater recruiting activity and more people with whom to work.

Two agencies with which I am personally familiar come to mind where there had been great emphasis on upgrading present organization with considerable success and a minimum of recruiting activity. Both agencies were leaders in their respective companies at one time. They ran into difficulty when certain of their big producers who they had personally developed stopped producing for various reasons. The reasons should not have come as a surprise. They happen all the time. The leading agent in one of these agencies was killed in an automobile accident at the age of 42. Another top agent in one of these agencies for family health reasons had to move to a different climate in another part of the country. Another decided to become a PPGA with another company while still another elected to take early retirement and as a result his very substantial production decreased dramatically. The home office took still another agent as an "advanced marketing consultant."

There may have been other problems in these agencies with which I am not familiar but the loss of so many big producers just had to be devastating. As a result both managers are now involved in a rebuilding program at a time in their careers when they would prefer to be thinking about doing some coasting.

I am not suggesting that it is not important and profitable to spend time helping established agents increase their production. It obviously is. But I submit that if this is done at the expense of adding new quality people in numbers on a consistent basis, the manager runs the risk of having his agency's production reduced dramatically by events over which he has no control. This can be avoided if he recognizes that there tends to be safety in numbers and approaches the recruiting part of the job on a realistic and practical basis.

There is still another reason why I feel the agency head should strive to develop "manpower." If the prime objective is to develop individuals, the manager is inclined to worry over his failures. He may think of them as a management failure. Perhaps in some instances this is true and certainly we should constantly review and attempt to improve our induction and training procedures. But also we should realize that *frailty* is a human characteristic. *Most people fail!* United States Department of Labor statistics report there is a 49.1% turnover in the manufacturing industry—one out of two. And most of them are union members.

And, finally, if the manager is placing his emphasis on the development of a limited number of individuals, there is a tendency to work too much with the status quo. If the manager thinks "manpower," he thinks in terms of change, which means constant recruiting and the agency is more alive and vibrant. New people stimulate the established organization and vice versa.

My conclusion after 30 years as an agency manager is this: To make an agency grow on a consistent basis over a long period of time, hire a goodly number of reasonably well-selected recruits each year, using all sources. Train them well with good field coaching at the start and do not forget them as they mature. But we must be prepared to accept a certain amount of failure and turnover—mentally, emotionally and financially. And keep right on hiring!

M #2 — MORALE

The second "M" is morale. A great deal has been said and a great deal written on this subject. Webster defines morale as "condition as affected by, or dependent upon, such moral or mental factors as zeal, spirit, hope and confidence." There is no doubt that a great deal of interrelation exists between these four factors. For example, an agent is certainly more zealous if his spirits are high and he has confidence in his own ability.

However, I think Webster's definition tells us quite specifically the areas of concern if a manager is to have high morale in his agency. So let's examine them. Hugh Bell also told me many years ago that managing an agency is basically very simple: All you have to do is hire a lot of good people and then keep them happy—and working! I am sure you will agree that this is a true observation. But it is much easier to say it than it is to do it, as we all know.

I have never found a method of successfully *making* agents work in our business over any sustained period of time. And I have tried many. The relationship which exists between an agent and his manager or general agent does not seem to lend itself to a strict employer-employee type of supervision. So we have to employ other methods and techniques. Of course, we can always terminate an agent's contract if he doesn't bring enough "zeal" to his work. And there are situations when this may well be the best approach. But this is the easy way and it really does not take much in the way of managerial skill and ability. The challenge of management is to help our associates approach their work with "spirit, hope and confidence" as Webster describes it. If these factors are generally positive within an agency, we have the essential requirements for good morale.

So how do we develop spirit? Competition can be very helpful. However, competition works best with people who are naturally competitive. It is easier to seek and recruit agents who enjoy and thrive on competition than it is to develop it in individuals who do not enjoy competing. In some instances they may prefer not to compete with other agents directly. But they can readily be encouraged to compete with themselves and their past accomplishments. I think spirit and the desire to compete go together and, if a manager can surround himself with a group of real competitors, it will go a long way toward building and maintaining good morale.

Hope is a factor in building morale that is often overlooked in working with agents. Yet we all know hope (anticipation) is necessary for our very existence. Without hope there would soon be a feeling that there is no reason to live. You know most managers left the agent's job—probably for a position as supervisor and then to the position of agency head. Did we not do this in anticipation of something different and hopefully better? We should never forget this when we are working with our associates.

Agents become bored doing the same thing over and over again, no matter how successful or unsuccessful they are. It is up to the manager to constantly challenge them, to give them hope, if you please, that they can do better than they are; that they can broaden, diversify and upgrade their markets; that they can improve their effectiveness and efficiency; that they are not in a rut in which they will be stuck for the next 20 or 30 years. This is a challenge to management, and the degree to which the manager is effective in responding to it will have a significant effect on the morale in his agency.

In another chapter I discuss the importance of encouraging attendance and participation at Million Dollar Round Table meetings, CLU Institutes, as well as local and state life underwriters association meetings. It is worth repeating as agents find these activities stimulating and informative. They broaden their outlook and enlarge their hope for the future which in turn improves their morale.

Psychologists tell us that man is the only animal that inherently fears his own species. Generally speaking, this is not a physical fear. It is a much more subtle fear but in some ways more difficult to understand and overcome. It is the fear of rejection—better known as "call reluctance" in the insurance business. All of us have it—it is just a matter of degree. And, generally speaking, it decreases in direct proportion as our self-confidence increases.

So here is another challenge to management—increase the self-confidence of your associates for they tend to call on the class of prospect with whom they feel secure, where they have confidence they won't be embarrassed or rejected. How does the manager do this? As I also mentioned in another chapter, encouraging them to increase their knowledge through CLU study and institutes; seminars, LUTC, company training courses, etc. All of these can be helpful depending upon the career stage of the agent. As knowledge increases, self-confidence grows and all of this tends to make a positive contribution to an agent's morale.

But there are other activities in which an agent can be encouraged to participate which will tend to increase his or her feeling of self-worth. Membership in a country club, or athletic club might do wonders for the agent's concept of himself and his potential. How about a Dale Carnegie course or Toastmasters Club? Membership and activity in service clubs such as Rotary, Lions, etc., can provide a nonthreatening growth experience. As a manager I used all of these with considerable success. And you can think of many more. We found that they did build confidence which as Webster says is one of the factors in morale—the second "M" in the four M's of management.

M #3 — MOMENTUM

The third "M" of management is momentum. Perhaps you have never thought of momentum as being as important to your agency's results as I believe it is. Read the next few pages with an open mind.

First of all, what is it? Let me give you an example of momentum and how powerful it is. I was born and reared in the State of Iowa. As a boy I have often watched a long freight train of 75 to 100 cars powered by one locomotive pull out of the station. The locomotive would spin its wheels as it attempted to get that long string of cars underway. It made me wonder if it could ever do it. But I have also seen similar length freight trains moving at 60+ miles per hour out on the prairie still powered by the one locomotive. What made the difference? Momentum!

Once you get a long freight train moving, it is relatively easy to keep it moving—and it is most difficult to stop! But once it slows down or stops, you again have the laborious task of getting it moving again. The conclusion is obvious—once you get it rolling, keep it rolling!

The same principle can be applied to many of the procedures and techniques of managing an agency. How is it created in an agency? Primarily by the manager. He sets the pace and his associates follow. If he lets down, they let down. If he becomes negative, they become negative. If he decides something cannot be done, they are quick to agree. On the other hand, if he is enthusiastic about the future and applies himself diligently to the job at hand, his associates tend to respond in kind.

I believe the manager must be consistently pushing in the direction he wants things to go, but first of all he should be certain *he knows exactly what he wants*—because there is a good chance he may get it!

The manager should be pushing the recruiting process all the time. In a large agency, obviously, he cannot do it all—but he should be on top of it and make certain that it does not break down. Nothing destroys momentum in an agency as inevitably as does failure to induct new sales associates. Every manager knows this but it is easy to let the pressure of other activities occupy his or her time. Before you know it, this all-important function is being neglected. Failure to recruit is insidious, but deadly in its effect on momentum. It may not show up for awhile but eventually it will. And by that time the "freight train is stopped" and you have to go through the travail of getting it moving again.

Momentum is very important in the recruiting process. When the manager decides he has some interest in a prospective recruit, he should get him busy doing things involving the agency—meeting agents, reviewing training courses, attending agency meetings, etc. In other words, keep the prospective agent so involved in the agency that he or she will have little time to consider other opportunities. All of this can be done without making a commitment prior to the final selection interview.

If you study your agency production records, you will quite likely discover an interesting cause and effect: the peaks and valleys in your agency's production can be related to your recruiting record. If you want a consistent growth pattern in the future with no loss in momentum, push the recruiting on a consistent basis.

The progress of the agents under contract can also play a significant role in an agency's momentum. It is the manager's responsibility to help agents continue to grow and develop, as I have previously mentioned. The greatest untapped resource in many agencies is the capacity for increased production from the established sales organization. But too often this does not happen. Agents are not challenged or pushed to even greater heights. They slow down and the agency slows down with them.

The manager once again is the key. He should work with these established associates personally on an individual or group basis. He should help them to be motivated and stimulated through additional training, direction and personal example. As they grow and develop, they help keep the agency moving ahead and provide a fertile seed bed into which to bring new inductees.

Another factor which can seriously affect an agency's momentum is the troublemaker who occasionally develops in an agency—particularly a large agency. In the agencies where I have personally known it to occur, it happened because the manager, to some extent at least, did not really know what was going on in his organization. These managers had achieved a fair amount of success and with this success developed an "executive complex." They had carried the delegation process to the point that they had lost contact and to a certain extent control of their agencies.

Now there is no question but that a manager has to delegate if he is ever to have an agency of any size. But it is my opinion that he should always have a good general idea of what is going on in all phases of the operation and not permit any one individual, valuable and capable as he may be, to become too important and too powerful. It can lead to serious problems and put production into a tailspin. It would make sense to terminate even a top producer before the manager should permit this to happen.

To avoid this possibility the manager should work extremely hard at maintaining an active grapevine. There are a few people in every agency who always know what is going on. The smart manager will cultivate them, take them to lunch occasionally, and because of this relationship the manager has a source of advance information regarding potential troublemakers and individual problems of all kinds. This will enable him or her to give them attention and hopefully resolve them before they reach the crisis stage. Utilizing an active agents advisory committee is a good way to have feedback regarding contemplated changes in agency policies and procedures. We all resist change, and quick changes which are not explained and understood can throw an agency off stride and destroy its momentum. An agency advisory committee can also be used as a training stage in the development of prospective new supervisors. It is a good opportunity to test judgment and leadership potential.

Most agencies have periods when the momentum has a natural tendency to slow down. One of these periods is December. Normally it is a great month for paid-for business as agents struggle to qualify for industry and company production clubs. However, written business tends to slack off. The result is a light paid-for in January and a slow start for the new year. One way to overcome this and maintain momentum is to have a sales campaign in December. Granted, it will not generate tremendous production. It will, however, stimulate enough associates (and particularly new agents) if properly promoted to enable the agency to move into the new year with a respectable volume of paid-for business and the important feeling that momentum has not been lost.

When agents return from industry meetings, company conferences and vacations there is a natural period of time before they can get back into production. The mail has piled up, policies to be delivered are stacked on their desks and it won't be easy to get back in the swing of making the calls and conducting the selling interviews which are necessary to make sales. One way to stimulate activity at this time is for the agency to send out extra direct mail for the agents who are gone, timed in such a way that the replies will be there when they return. This will tend to stimulate them to make calls which they would not otherwise make. As a result they will make the transition into new sales activity sooner and more effectively than might otherwise be the case.

As I have indicated, momentum can be an important asset in your agency in many ways. It is important that this be recognized and that consistent efforts be made to use it effectively.

M #4 — MOTIVATION

The fourth "M" I want to discuss is motivation. Once again let's start by defining what it is. There are numerous definitions we could use but in simplest terms it can be described as "the force which causes people to do things." Psychologists tell us that all activity is self-motivated and goal-directed. In other words, none of us does *anything* without a specific reason for doing it.

We need also to keep in mind that no one does very much of anything simply because someone else wants him or her to do it. We may respond, but not just because the other person wanted us to—but rather because we wanted his approval. So it actually becomes a goal for us—the goal being approval. Perhaps you may think I am just indulging in semantics, but if you analyze closely what I have said, there is a significant difference. The difference substantiates my previous point that in the final analysis all activity is self-motivated and goal-directed. The manager really cannot "motivate" his associates to do what he wants them to do. Instead he has to help them to motivate themselves in terms of their own self-interest.

Where does it start? As always, with the manager. But who motivates the manager? The home office tries and in some instances, I am sure, quite successfully. But the more successful managers and general agents have the capacity for self-motivation and all of us should recognize its importance. It is difficult for the manager to help others become motivated if he is not motivated himself.

How can managers motivate themselves? The best method I can recommend from experience is to put yourself on the spot. Tell your associates, your home office, your spouse, etc., what your goals are. Don't kid yourself! Make them realistic but publicize them sufficiently so that failure to reach them—or at least come very close—will be a source of embarrassment. The fear of failure is often a greater source of motivation than is the desire for success. I know it is with me. But first you may have to *risk failure* by putting yourself on the spot before becoming motivated by fear of failure.

Assuming we are motivated, how do we motivate our associates to help us reach *our* goals? As I have already stated, we can only do this to the extent that they want to *please* us. A better approach is to strive to motivate them in terms of their own desires and self-interest. To be specific, an agent might not be particularly interested in having the agency win a President's Citation. But he might like the idea of taking his spouse or girlfriend to the big dinner-dance to which he will be invited if the agency is a winner.

An effective technique is to encourage agents to constantly improve their standard of living, even to going in debt within reasonable limitations. As I have mentioned previously, joining a country club or athletic club is good business in several ways. There are many ideas that can be planted in an associate's mind—or perhaps his spouse's mind—which will become built-in motivation for ever-increasing production and the income that goes with it—for a new home, a new car, travel, to name a few. This is not a new idea, of course, but it is important not to forget that it still works if it is used consistently and not too obviously.

It is desirable to create "situations" within an agency which tend to provide motivation in the direction the manager wants things to go. For example, you might consider asking a good producing agent who is also a good student and a CLU to help promote the CLU program within the agency. This serves two purposes. First, it makes the agent feel important and improves his morale. Secondly, and more important, it has a good chance of being effective because as an agent it is far easier and in many instances more effective for an agent to challenge supervisors and other agents to become CLUs. Obviously he has no ulterior motive as someone in management might be thought to have. Furthermore, he is not inhibited from suggesting—even demanding—that students give their studies the necessary time and energy despite a concern that their production might be adversely affected.

Office allocation can be used very successfully as a built-in motivator. I am sure those managers who do this have a well-publicized set of rules which is distributed in advance of the start of the qualifying period, which normally would be the calendar year. The rules should be designed to keep office changes to a minimum while at the same time providing adequate motivation. If you do not have such a system, I suggest you seriously consider installing one. If you already have one in place, you might want to review it to determine if it is up-to-date and serving the purpose for which it was designed.

Most agencies recognize an "Agent of the Year" on an annual basis. I know many local general agents and managers associations sponsor an annual "Agent of the Year" banquet. The opportunity to compete for such recognition in front of one's peers can be a very positive form of motivation. However, the basis for selecting the agency winner should be well-designed and consistently promoted in order that the maximum in motivation can be obtained.

If you feel, as I do, that competition with adequate recognition to the winners is good for morale, here is another idea to consider, if you have 35 or more agents. The objective is to have more competitive races and more opportunities for year-end recognition. The National Football League and Major League Baseball both use this idea very successfully. You might want to consider dividing your agency into three competitive groups—heavyweights, light heavyweights, and middleweights. Previous production results would be the basis for assignment to a group, with all new agents in the middleweight category. This would enable the agency to recognize three leaders at year-end after, hopefully, having had three close races with fairly broad participation. The winner of each of the two lower groups would automatically move up to the next group. This would tend to provide considerable depth in your recognition program with greater overall interest and participation.

Most agencies recognize an "Agent of the Month" on some basis. If you are not now doing so, I would encourage you to give the idea serious consideration. There are many ways to recognize the monthly leader—picture in the lobby, plaque, business gift (extra direct mail, postage, magazine subscriptions), etc. Another idea is for the manager and his spouse to personally entertain the winner at dinner with cocktails in the manager's home prior to dining. This has several advantages: it enables the manager and his spouse to spend time on a social basis with the leading agents in the agency without running the risk of being accused of favoritism. Furthermore, a personal relationship can be established in this setting perhaps better than would be possible in the office. In addition, it gives the spouses an opportunity to know each other and feel more a part of the agency. It is my experience that it is quite effective and I recommend you consider adopting it as part of your recognition and morale-building program.

I think it is desirable that the manager constantly promote the idea that "it is fun to be in our business." I believe that and I always have. You can make as much money as you want by helping people and in doing so derive the deep personal satisfaction everyone needs for real happiness. The manager also must recognize the desire all of us have to feel we are making progress. The need for self-improvement is vital to morale and motivation. Set a good example and others will follow.

I have discussed four M's of management. There are other factors with which managers must be concerned but it is my belief that these are the most important: first, manpower—it is the name of the game; second, morale—its ingredients are zeal, spirit, hope, and confidence; third, momentum—its significance is easy to overlook until an agency is in trouble; and finally, motivation—the force which causes people to do things. May I remind you, however, that no matter how effective you may be in all of these areas, you will still have troubles and problems. Why? Because you are working with people. It is as simple as that.

Years ago I picked up a bit of philosophy which has helped me when I become frustrated with the way things are going. Perhaps it will be helpful to you. It goes like this:

Look for more troubles. Be thankful for the troubles of your job. They contribute greatly to your income and if it were not for the things that go wrong, the difficult people you have to deal with, and the problems and unpleasantness of your working day, someone could be found to handle your job at half of what you are being paid.

It takes intelligence, resourcefulness, patience, tact and courage to meet the problems of any important job. That is why you hold your present position and may be the reason you are not holding down an even more important one. If all of us would look for more troubles and learn to handle them cheerfully and with good judgment as opportunities rather than irritations, we would find ourselves getting ahead at a surprising rate. For it is a fact that there are plenty of big jobs waiting for men and women who are not afraid of the troubles connected with them.

* * *

5.

AGENT-MANAGER RELATIONSHIPS

In this chapter I will discuss the job of being an agency head from the standpoint of the relationships which develop between agents and manager. These ideas and concepts are based on my experience of managing the same agency in the same city for the same company for 30 years to the day.

Some of you may remember a Burt Bacharach song entitled "Alfie." The opening words of that song are: "What's it all about, Alfie! Is it just for the moment we live? What's it all about when you sort it out, Alfie? Are we meant to take more than we give?"

I believe that these are challenging questions, and ultimately each one of us will answer them in his or her own way. The songwriter asks what "it" is all about. But "it" is a very unspecific word. "It" can mean almost anything we want it to mean. For example, "it" could refer to life, success (whatever that is), personal satisfaction, happiness, good health or maybe a combination of all five.

I believe that good relationships are what "it" is all about. Good relationships—a phrase that we hear used quite often these days.

What is a good relationship? I am sure everyone could come up with his or her definition. However, I suspect that they would not be too dissimilar if we were to compare them. So that we are on common ground, let me give you mine:

A good relationship is one in which two or more individuals contribute on a sustaining basis to the happiness, accomplishments *or* feelings of personal worth of each other. A superior relationship is one in which two or more individuals contribute to each other on a sustaining basis in all three of these areas. I am not suggesting that this is a perfect definition, but it is a point of departure from which we can explore many other areas of human communication.

It is my opinion that there are four requirements—or ingredients—of a good relationship. They are vital to the success of a manager or general agent. (I believe they are also vital to a successful marriage and a healthy, happy, and rewarding life!)

TRUST—THE MOST IMPORTANT INGREDIENT

The first and most important ingredient in any relationship is trust. It is the foundation and an absolute must! A manager simply cannot afford to hire or keep associates whom he cannot trust 100 percent. Sooner or later he will pay the price if he keeps untrustworthy people. I don't care how much they produce.

If you have anyone in your agency who cannot be trusted, I encourage you to figure out a way to get rid of him or her without delay. You can never have a lasting relationship with such a person, and it will only be a matter of time until you regret having tolerated the lack of the one quality that is imperative. I've had some unfortunate personal experiences both in and out of the insurance business where I tried to build a relationship with people who were not completely trustworthy, and I also know of many situations in my company where the need for mutual trust was compromised. In each instance the manager paid dearly. I'm sure most of you know from personal experience what I am talking about.

Just as the manager must have associates who can be trusted, they also must know that he is totally trustworthy in his relationships with them, the home office and the policyowners. For example: the manager should never make a promise which he or she does not keep. This is particularly true in the area of recognition programs including office space and secretarial assistance. The agent loses confidence in a manager who describes what he will do for him if his production reaches a certain level and then doesn't deliver.

I know a manager who promoted qualification to attend a conference at Las Vegas. Near the end of the qualifying period the announcement was made that the conference would be moved to Monterey. Monterey is a delightful spot but not nearly as attractive to agents on the West Coast and particularly in California, where a high percentage of the potential qualifiers lived. They had really looked forward to Las Vegas. The agents were advised that the change of location was made for "budgetary reasons." In this instance the manager may have saved money but I wonder if it was worth the loss of credibility with his associates.

The manager must set a personal example of trustworthiness in his dealings with the home office and policyowners. For example, he should never withhold pertinent information from the underwriting department or any other department. If the agents observe him doing this, they draw the obvious conclusion that the manager is untrustworthy. The same thing applies to policyowners. The manager must be aboveboard in all his actions if he expects his agents to trust him.

It is important that the manager do his level best to treat all associates fairly. Granted that this is a subjective decision, if he or she makes a concerted effort in this direction the reaction is very likely to be positive. This does not mean that all agents should be treated equally. The super agents naturally should receive better treatment. They have earned it. However, if all agents of approximately the same level of production and years of service are treated essentially the same, the manager will be perceived as fair and trustworthy.

It is essential that new agents know exactly what they can expect when they join the agency. This includes the training and field assistance they can expect as well as secretarial assistance, direct mail, telephone, postage, etc. All of this information should be reduced to writing and presented at a mutual obligations interview prior to the agent coming under contract. The manager must then follow through with what he has agreed to do if he wants to maintain the agent's confidence and trust.

Finally, in all his relationships the manager is challenged to set an example of honesty and integrity that his associates will want to emulate. People are always more inclined to do what they observe than they are to do what they hear.

ACCEPTANCE—PLUS ADJUSTMENT

The second ingredient for a good relationship is acceptance. There are all kinds of people in the world, and a large life insurance agency is a cross section of all of those different kinds of people, each with their own personal problems.

Many members of the Seattle Agency had been with me more than 20 years. During my last two years as manager, we had our share of sadness:

- An agent who had been with the agency 28 years committed suicide very unexpectedly.

- An agent who had been with the agency 29 years died of cancer.

- An agent with 22 years in the agency had a heart attack and then a four-way bypass operation.

- An agent who had been with us for 26 years and another who had been with us 15 years both had wives die of cancer. They both took it very hard.

Just as these events are happening all the time in our communities, they are happening in our agencies. Managers must learn to accept and work with many different problems and many kinds of people if they are to maintain their physical and emotional health.

Some of the different kinds of people a manager might have are:

- *Agents they don't particularly like.* Do you have any? I did, and some of them were substantial producers. But they were honest and competent, and I accepted them.

- *Agents who are totally unappreciative of anything anyone does to help them.* Do you have any of them? I did. But they, too, were honest, competent, and productive, and I learned to accept their lack of consideration and sometimes downright rudeness.

- *Agents who work on the fringe of their potential.* Do you have any who fall into this category? I did, and they were very frustrating to me. I tried everything I had heard and read to motivate them, but to no avail. So I must accept what the psychologists tell us and which I have mentioned elsewhere in this book: "No one really motivates someone else. All motivation is self-motivation." John Wooden, the great basketball coach at UCLA whose teams won 10 National Championships, once said, "I haven't motivated a basketball player in my life. I may have contributed to molding them into a team role, but if the players I recruit aren't already motivated, then I've recruited the wrong guys." I think this is great advice for the agency manager. Recruit motivated people! The agents in the Seattle Agency who operated well below their potential were honest. They wrote good business and they serviced it well. They never made the Million Dollar Round Table and they never will. Most larger agencies have agents who fall in that category. For his own peace of mind, the manager must accept them for what they are. The time may come—and it may be sooner than the manager would like to think—when he cannot afford to provide them with office space. But who knows, maybe they will rise to the challenge and meet reasonable production standards in order to maintain space in the agency office.

- *Agents who no longer attend agency meetings consistently.* Do you have any? I did. And it irritated the devil out of me. There was a time years ago when I simply would not have tolerated it. But there comes a time when the manager must accept the fact that "the kids have grown up." New recruits and 25-year veterans are not attracted to the same meeting agenda. Material for various levels of knowledge and expertise must be made available and it is the manager's responsibility to figure out the best way to do it. Furthermore, the manager must also accept the fact that a key appointment on a large case may be more important to an established agent than an agency meeting, no matter how much time and effort the manager may have spent in its preparation.

- *Ex-associates who have left the agency for various reasons.* Do you have any of these? I'm sure I have had more than my share. The manager simply must accept that most people do not succeed, no matter what their field of endeavor. Failure in our business just seems to be more common than in other fields because the insurance business is one of the few businesses that keeps records and publicizes them. (As an aside we should bear in mind that the medical, dental, and law professions have a high degree of failure *in college*. I am referring to all the college students who take premed and prelaw and *drop out* along the way.)

I am referring not only to the failures the manager has to terminate for lack of production after all those hours of work, but also the successful people who leave for various reasons. Nine associates left the Seattle Agency to become managers for Prudential—that averages almost one every three years. A great deal of work and effort went into their development. Although I was happy to see them leave and do well, there were times when in all honesty I admit to having had some ambivalent feelings. I had other successful agents leave the agency for various reasons—family problems, health problems, ego problems (they wanted their own shops but never could qualify to be Prudential managers).

I have had managers in other cities call me when they lost a top agent. They wanted my advice. I would tell them, "I've lost more good agents than you will probably ever lose—I have been in the business so many years. The only answer is to get busy recruiting his or her replacement—and the sooner the better!" We can't keep them all, no matter how hard we try. Our only choice is to accept his or her leaving as one of the vicissitudes of agency building. And get on with the job!

It is important, incidentally, that the departure be as friendly as possible. It is in the manager's best interest to maintain as good a relationship as possible. Perhaps the departing agent won't replace quite as much business as he would if there were hard feelings. Besides, bitter feelings cause ulcers. Furthermore, there is always the possibility that the new connection may not work out and he might want to come back. I have had agents do just that. I would also encourage you to keep in mind what Napoleon Hill wrote in his great book *Think and Grow Rich*: "Every hardship, failure or adversity brings with it the seed of an equivalent or greater benefit." I believe that. I have seen it happen many times in my life and the lives of my associates.

- *Home office people who make errors of various kinds that contribute negatively to agency efficiency and morale.* Has this ever happened to you? It has happened to me many times. But, on the other hand, home office people are very helpful on many occasions. The manager should accept the fact that they don't deliberately mess up. If he believes that, gives them the benefit of the doubt when they make a mistake, and goes out of his way to show appreciation when they are particularly helpful, the overall results will be more effective and productive for all concerned.

- *Supervisors who don't do things exactly the way we used to do them.* It is easy for all of us to believe there is a right way and a wrong way to perform most tasks. And to a certain extent that may be true. But I have alwyas felt that agency management is not an exact science. It is an art. There are many variations on how to perform the job of agency supervisor. I believe the manager should accept this and allow his supervisors the freedom to grow and develop within the framework of an overall agency philosophy.

- *Yourself.* Do you accept yourself? Do you recognize and accept your strong points and limitations? No manager is equally strong in all areas of agency management. The manager should accept this and staff his agency accordingly. For example, some managers may not be strong in the technical field. Advanced marketing may not be their strength. If this is so, each must develop a staff person to meet this need while the manager concentrates on his strength, which might be one-on-one relationships, recruiting, goal-setting, etc. Not only is this necessary to help the agency to grow, but also from a health standpoint it is good for the manager to accept his limitations.

There are other areas that require the manager's acceptance and adjustment. Changes in the marketplace is an example. There is nothing we can do about them. They happen. But there is a market out there for the products you have to sell, no matter what company you represent. It is up to the field management to accept that as a fact and transform that acceptance into positive results in their individual agencies.

MUTUAL RESPECT

A third ingredient in a good relationship is mutual respect. I am sure you share my belief that it is more important for a manager's associates to respect him than like him; of course, it is better if they do both. I have already stated that I had members of the Seattle Agency whom I did not particularly like. But I did not have any for whom I did not have a fair degree of respect, for one reason or another. Obviously, there are some whom I respected more than others, but production was only one of the factors I used in making that determination.

Here are some of the areas the manager might consider when measuring the respect he has for an agent:

1. Production. This cannot be ignored. In fact it is the bottom line.

2. Personal growth and development (MDRT, CLU, etc.). The manager should have a great deal of respect for agents who don't have much going for them when they start out, but who continue to get better through professional studies, consistent effort, etc.

3. Quality of personal and family life (contribution to church, synagogue and community activities).

4. Industry and civic involvement.

5. Contribution and loyalty to the agency and company.

6. Quality of business and service rendered to the clients.

7. Integrity in the way the agent conducts his business. Although I have this at the bottom of the list, I believe it is a very important quality. Webster defines integrity as "unimpaired moral principles" and that sums up in three words a quality that deserves the manager's highest respect.

The manager does not have to have respect for any agent in *all* these areas to have a worthwhile relationship, but he should respect him or her in several. If production is the only quality the manager respects, he is operating on shaky ground. Of course, if an agent isn't making a decent living—especially if he or she has a family to support—it is difficult to have much respect, no matter how strong the agent is in the other areas. And, as I have already mentioned, if production doesn't measure up, the manager may be forced to conclude that he cannot afford to provide the agent with office space.

If the manager cannot respect an associate, he should figure out a way to get him or her out of the agency. In the long run, such a person can never be an asset.

Respect goes both ways, so here are some places where managers can earn the respect of their agency associates:

1. Manage a successful agency, according to company standards. This is the manager's bottom line. Bob Beck, Chairman and Chief Executive Officer of the

Prudential Insurance Company of America, refers to the "irrefutable logic of results."

2. Concentrate on personal growth. Surveys have indicated that many agents feel that they have "outgrown" their managers. He should set a good example of study and work habits. CLU studies are, of course, a must. The Agency Management Training Course has to be high on the list for any agency head who has not already completed it.

3. Have integrity in all he says and does. I have already defined integrity, which says it all.

4. Contribute to his agent's success—knowledge, skills, backup services, prestige with home office. Be available to provide help and encouragement.

5. Be involved in industry and community affairs. Agents like to identify with an agency head who is respected in the community and by his peers and competitors.

Agents do not have to like their manager or general agent, but to have an effective relationship they must respect him. The manager must never forget, however, that he has to *earn* their respect. Having the title of manager does not by itself bring respect. Respect comes from the manner in which he conducts himself daily, the example he sets in all areas, and the success of his agency.

COMMUNICATION—VERBAL AND NONVERBAL

The fourth ingredient for a good relationship is communication, of which there are two kinds:

1. *Verbal communication* is what we are most familiar with. Among the manager's responsibilities is to be available when an agent wants to talk. This isn't easy

to do in a large agency but the manager must work at it constantly. He must strive to be perceptive of an agent's moods (most agents have varying periods of ups and downs). He must listen to his agents and be a good sounding board. He should never let any extensive period pass without having some direct contact with each associate. Having some method of monitoring this activity is essential. Relying on memory cannot be depended upon.

2. *Nonverbal communication* encompasses a number of areas. The manager should never minimize in his mind the importance of these forms of communication in an agency:

   - *Agency Philosophy*—It is the manager's responsibility to communicate the agency's goals and markets so that the agents know where they fit in. (This is developed in the chapter on "What Kind of Agency.")

   - *Recognition Programs*—There are numerous bases for giving recognition in an agency. Whatever method or methods are used become nonverbal methods of communication that the manager considers important. For example, if persistency is highlighted the agents will soon accept the fact that the manager is interested in quality business. Lives, commissions, volume, premium are all possibilities that the agency can emphasize for the same purpose. If product diversification is an agency goal, recognition programs can also be designed to communicate that goal. The manager should review his or her recognition programs periodically to make certain that they are communicating the goals and standards he wishes to emphasize.

   - *Office Space Allocation Rules*—Agents respond to this form of communication even when it may be difficult to have personal discussions with them. There are numerous ways to use office allocation as a communicator. For example, the manager can require certain levels of persistency, lives, commissions, etc., to qualify for certain types of office space, or a combination of two or more. However, it is important that the office allocation rules be distributed well in advance of the qualifying period and every effort made to eliminate any chance for misunderstandings. Furthermore, too many changes in the rules are not advisable. The agents will react more favorably to a consistent approach from year to year. Of course, it is absolutely essential that the rules be administered exactly as published with no exceptions.

- *Secretarial Allowances*—Essentially the manager can use the same approach as he does for office allocation. However, if he wants to communicate a slightly different message for whatever reason, he can use his rules for secretarial allowance for this purpose. But it is imperative that the two sets of rules not be in conflict and that both sets of rules be thoroughly understood and impartially administered.

A relationship established in a nonverbal manner may enhance an agent's production when all other forms of communication are for the most part ineffective.

In summary, here are some key points in the establishment of good communications.

- Be available.
- Be interested.
- Be a good listener. Listen with your eyes!
- Be consistent.
- Be dependable.

- Be open and clear in defining your expectations and what is important.
- Be honest and fair in all you say and do.

As you think about the associates with whom you have the closest relationships, you will doubtless discover that you not only enjoy each other's company, but you are also contributing substantially to each other's accomplishments. At the same time you are developing a feeling of greater personal worth.

Most managers and general agents will probably have some associates whose principal—and maybe only—contribution is production. I know I did. It is important that the manager understand the basis of their relationship with this kind of associate. We must recognize that we cannot change him or her and to strive for a closer relationship will probably be counterproductive (in the truest sense of the word) and perhaps emotionally upsetting.

The concepts I have outlined here are probably more immediately useful to the manager or general agent with an established agency and a number of associates already under contract. But they can still be helpful to those who have relatively small operations but plan to grow. Chances are that if you develop an agency of some size, no matter how selective you strive to be, you eventually will have a cross section of humanity with all the different problems and personalities that entails. It is unlikely you will have superior relationships with all of your associates.

The challenge to all of us is to understand and accept the fact that good relationships are vital to our accomplishments and that we must learn to work with all kinds of people and all kinds of problems. It isn't easy, but it can be done, and the awards in personal satisfaction and income are substantial.

I am sure most of you are familiar with I Corinthians 13:4-7 from the Holy Bible. This is the greatest statement of love, which is at the heart of all superior relationships. I will paraphrase by inserting the words "good agency management" whenever "love" appears:

> Good agency management is patient, good agency management is kind. It does not envy, it does not boast. It is not proud. It is not rude, it is not self-seeking. It is not easily angered, it keeps no records of wrongs. Good agency management does not delight in evil, but rejoices with the truth. It always protects, always trusts, always hopes, always perseveres.

* * *

6.

SELF-IMPOSED LIMITATIONS

The basic premise of this chapter is that all of us can do more than we are doing—most people far more. We have not reached our full potential. To say it still another way, "Nothing is as good as it can be"—and that includes each one of us.

Before I become specific, I would like to observe that limitations are not overcome overnight. All of us have to work at them. Richard Bach, in his delightful book, *Jonathan Livingston Seagull,* expressed it so well: "It happened just a week later. Fletcher Lynn Seagull snapped hard to the left at something over 200 miles an hour into a cliff of solid granite. It was for him as though the rock were a giant hard door into another world. A burst of fear and shock and black as he hit and then he was adrift in a strange, strange sky. Forgetting; remembering; forgetting. Afraid and sad and sorry. Terribly sorry, the voice came to him as it had on the first day he met Jonathan Livingston Seagull. 'The trick, Fletcher, is that we are trying to overcome our limitations in order. Patiently. We don't tackle flying through solid rock until later in the program.' "

The moral in the excerpt is this: we cannot do it all—just like that! But the implication is that it can be achieved—any reasonable goal, if we work at it in order, patiently.

I subscribe to this premise—but in order to work intelligently we must determine what our long-range goals are. We don't want to pour out our lives in some form of endeavor and then when it is too late discover that what we have been working for is not what we want at all. As someone once said, "Be careful what you ask for because you may get it."

Unfortunately, many people do not really know what they want. They are confused about their goals. They are like the captain of a ship who sets out to sea with no destination in mind. Sounds foolish, doesn't it? But no more foolish than for a man or woman not to have a goal for his or her life. Unfortunately, too many people do not. Consequently it is not surprising that they accomplish very little with their lives in comparison with their potential.

Having a well thought out objective does not assure that it will be reached. It is, however, the first step and extremely important. There are limitations for all of us which militate against the achievement of long-range goals. It is my opinion, however, that these are self-imposed limitations and for the most part are within our power to overcome.

ATTITUDE

The first limitation is attitude—we don't think we can do it, whatever it is—and we are right!

There is a tremendous difference between the production of the top agents or agencies of any company as compared with the production of the "average" agent or agency in the same company. Is it basic ability that makes the difference? Perhaps to a certain extent—but attitude plays a big role. The leaders *believe* they can do it. There is the key difference!

A number of years ago, I attended the Seattle Life Underwriters Association October meeting with a group of my Prudential associates. The speaker was an agent from San Francisco who was on schedule to pay for $12,000,000 of business. He said that his goal at the beginning of the year was to pay for $1,000,000 a month. He had analyzed his records and determined how many cases he would need to achieve that objective. As I recall the number was 30 cases a month with an average size of slightly less than $35,000. He believed at the beginning of the year that he was capable of achieving that level of production and after 10 months he was slightly ahead of schedule.

When we returned to the office I overheard two of my associates discussing the speaker's fabulous production. One of them said, "You know I could never produce at that level. I can't even conceive of anyone writing that volume of business!" And then the other agent made an extremely sage observation when he said, "And you know, Vic, you have just stated the primary reason *you* will never do it. You cannot conceive it as being possible."

Almost 50 years ago in his classic book *Think and Grow Rich,* Napoleon Hill wrote, "Whatever the mind of man can conceive and believe, it can achieve." Do you believe that? I do and I know it has been helpful many times in my life as well as in the lives of many of my associates. A classic example was the U.S. Hockey Team's defeat of the Russian team at the 1980 Olympic Games. They believed they could win and although they were expected to lose by just about everyone, they pulled off one of the greatest upsets in the history of Olympic competition. The sports world is replete with countless stories of athletic contests where a winning attitude made the difference in turning what was generally considered certain defeat into a magnificent victory. Yes, outstandingly successful people in every field of endeavor have a positive, success-oriented attitude. The record is so convincing that I would hope you would agree that its overwhelming importance cannot be questioned.

Of course, this is not a new concept. But, unfortunately, many people still do not accept it as they should. They may give lip service to the idea but that is all. How about you? Are you prepared to accept as a possibility that your attitude leaves something to be desired? Could it be a self-imposed limitation over which you have considerable control? And now the key question: Would you like to change it?

Some suggestions on how you can change your attitude —none new:

- Strive to get a bigger concept of your potential.

- Concentrate on thinking bigger. Make a concerted effort in this direction.

- Concentrate on feeding positive thoughts into your mind on a regular basis. There are many books that you can read that can provide positive input.

- Affirm your goals to yourself and to others. Do it every day.

- Accept the truism that "we become what we think about."

Many who read this won't take it seriously—won't do anything about it. But that is unfortunate for them—because it works. I know from personal experience and observation.

Some other suggestions:

- Avoid negative thinkers and negative thoughts.

- Concentrate on spending your time with successful, positive people.

- Attend life underwriters association meetings, local general agents and managers meetings, sales congresses, MDRT annual meetings, CLU institutes, LAMP meetings.

- Form study groups within or outside your company.

- In other words, *work at improving your attitude!*

Knowledge is power—but it is also a great attitude adjuster. This is particularly true if you concentrate on using the knowledge you acquire to enhance your professional effectiveness. (More on this later.) Become a student of the business—but don't overdo it. Try to keep everything in proper perspective, including a proper balance between your business and personal life.

EXPENDING EFFORT

The second limitation is in the amount of effort-work-drive you are willing to expend.

We have—each one of us—either what we really want out of life, or we should be in the process of acquiring it! (Would you please read that sentence again. It is very important!) Some people do not really want very much out of life, for whatever reason, and that is exactly what they will get. Consistent effort is *always* rewarded and we always pay the price for lack of effort. You all know this—you have observed it in others and undoubtedly experienced it personally. But as I heard Red Motley, former President of the U.S. Chamber of Commerce, say many years ago, "Nobody is smart enough to remember everything he or she knows." So we need to be reminded—and that is what I hope this book is doing for its readers.

There is a story about a young man who was always late for work. One morning the boss said to him, "Young man, do you know what time we start work around here?" The young man replied, "No, I really don't. They are always at it when I get here." And that is the way it is with the leaders in our business—they are always at it—making the calls, seeing the people and doing the work. The losers are somewhere else.

Some people say they do not want to "work all the time." That is nothing but a rationalization. Very vew people in or out of the insurance business are even close to overworking, and they are all doing very well. It is a matter of time control.

There are "majors" and "minors" in every type of work. Generally speaking, the majors are the more *creative* aspects of the job (for example, prospecting for the agent, recruiting for the manager). Whether you are an agent or manager you do not need someone else to figure out for you what your most important duties are. You already know. But more than likely they are not the part of the job that you enjoy the most. In fact, the reverse may be true. But you must discipline yourself to do these things first. That is the secret of time control.

The "minors" of the job—"work processing" of all kinds—will tend to take care of themselves. In many instances you can and should delegate much of this kind of work to others. But if this is not possible for whatever reason, it is imperative that you prioritize your responsibilities, establish a schedule and then follow it religiously.

Confucius said, "He who justifies does not convince." People are not impressed when you say you are working "too hard." In most instances it simply will not sell. Always remember that no one is really interested in hearing *why* you are not getting the job done (not even your spouse). If you are successful, they will enjoy hearing *what* you are doing, *how* you are doing it, and perhaps *why*—but *not* why you are *not*!

It is my conviction that the primary purpose of just about all excuses for not working is to rationalize lack of effort. This, then, becomes another self-imposed limitation. And one which we can readily do something about.

KNOWLEDGE

The third limitation is in the area of knowledge.

It is important to understand and accept that the only knowledge with any *practical* value is that knowledge we use. Of course, there are many reasons to acquire knowledge of all kinds. Certainly a degree in liberal arts makes the graduate a "more rounded" human being. There is a certain challenge in acquiring knowledge in many diverse fields. It improves our conversation, makes us more interesting people and gives us a great deal of personal satisfaction.

But insofar as our own profession is concerned, knowledge should be acquired for the specific purpose of improving our professional competence. Many times I have observed individuals complete courses of various kinds, including CLU work, which considerably enhance their technical competence. As a result, they were *capable* of upgrading their markets, working in more advanced fields and by so doing increasing their income substantially. *But, too often, nothing happened.* They continued to work in the same basic market, just as if they had never qualified themselves to prospect upwards. Not only is this not very good judgment but to a certain extent it is a waste of time and effort.

There is plenty of opportunity to acquire knowledge in this business—company courses, LUTC basic and advanced, CLU designation and degree work, CFP, ChFC, MDRT, LAMP, AMTC, CLU Institutes, etc. They are familiar to all of us. However, the purpose of all knowledge and training should be a behavioral change. Action is a must, once you acquire additional knowledge. However, you should use it intelligently—to develop and expand your professional skills, to work smarter and more effectively.

A woman I know is determined to be the best-informed person anywhere about life insurance and financial planning. She has licenses permitting her to sell almost anything; she has passed all the LUTC courses, has achieved her CLU designation and is now working on her ChFC. But she isn't selling enough life insurance or anything else to keep her head above water financially. Until she achieves a balance between *learning* and *doing*, she is on her way to becoming the most talented financial planner in the unemployment line.

I believe you will agree that there is plenty of knowledge available in the insurance business and it is expanding at an accelerating pace. The extent to which you acquire it and use it in adequate amounts is a self-imposed limitation. For you can do something about it if you want to. The knowledge is available and the prospects out there are waiting to hear your story.

SKILL

The fourth limitation is in the area of skill. What are you doing to improve your skills? Or do you believe you are a master salesperson? How about your recruiting presentation? How long since you tried to make it more effective? Maybe you are in a great big rut and don't know it. It may be a comfortable rut—but it still could be a rut!

Someone once said, "You can't escape from a prison if you don't know you are in one." People can be in ruts which are, in effect, prisons and they do not know it. Unwillingness to work at self-improvement of skill is probably the most widespread self-imposed limitation. As your skill increases, you become more effective, results bring increased confidence and confidence makes you more effective.

Professional athletes spend a great deal of time working at skill. In April of 1967, I was privileged to attend three days of the Masters Golf Tournament in Augusta, Georgia. Gary

Player, one of the greatest golfers on the PGA Tour at that time, had had a poor putting round the second day of the four-day tournament. Immediately after he finished his round he and his caddy headed straight for the putting green. He instructed his caddy to place four balls some eight to 10 feet from one of the holes. He proceeded to deliberately stroke the four balls toward the cup one at a time. The caddy would knock them back to him and he would do it again. I was watching the players putt out on the 18th green and keeping an eye on Player as he practiced 10-foot putts. Would you believe he kept at it for one full hour before he was satisfied? He didn't win the Masters that year, but don't you know a 10-foot putt looked mighty familiar the next day!

That is a typical example of a professional athlete drilling for skill. How about you? How long since you put a presentation on an audio-video and then analyzed it with an associate as to how you might improve? How often do you practice a sales presentation before making that important call? Or do you just "shoot from the hip"?

Suppose someone offered you $2,000 to make a talk to a small group two weeks from tonight on a subject relating to insurance—with the understanding, however, that you would receive nothing if the group did not feel you did a good job. Would you practice? Would you have someone listen to you in advance? Would you put your presentation on audio-video? Of course you would! Does it make any sense, then, to "wing it" on a sales call which could readily be worth $2,000 or more? Or, if you are a manager, not to prepare and practice for the recruiting presentation which might attract a multi-million dollar producer to your agency?

There are many ways to improve your skill. I have already touched on the use of audio-video as a means of evaluating and improving your presentations. Role playing with an associate or spouse is excellent. The Agency Management Training Course, which is basically a skill-building course for agency managers and general agents, uses role playing at just about every session to build skill. As a former moderator and student of this course, I know it works.

There are many excellent cassettes available. Tapes from MDRT annual meetings, CLU Institutes, LAMP meetings, etc., are excellent skill-building tools. All you have to do is take the time to listen to them and then apply what you learn.

Surely you must recognize that you can improve your skill if you dedicate yourself to doing so. And if you do not—it is a self-imposed limitation.

FAITH

The fifth limitation is *in the area of faith.* There are three different kinds of faith and each plays an important role in our lives. The first is faith in a "Supreme Being"—Almighty God to most of us. This is the root of all faith. A second kind is faith in others—family, associates, friends, company, business. The third kind is faith in oneself—first, as a human being and second, as having what it takes to be successful in one's chosen field.

It isn't easy to cope with the problems of a career in life insurance. There are many high moments and, of course, the long-range potential is second to none. But, as we all know, insurance people are constantly experiencing rejection and disappointment. It comes with the territory, as Willie Loman said in *Death of a Salesman,* particularly in the early years. Most of us at one or more times in our business career have probably found ourselves sufficiently discouraged and frustrated that we have given casual consideration at least to giving up and finding an "easier" way to make a living. I know I did in my first year.

I still have a vivid memory of a Sunday afternoon when I was giving serious consideration to leaving the business and going to college. I was 29 years old and had been an agent for almost 12 months. My production overall had been quite good. However, for the past month I had been in the middle of my first slump and to say the least I was not finding it enjoyable.

I entered the business immediately after being discharged from the U.S. Navy in 1945, where I had served for 6½ years. My background qualifications for success were not outstanding and I was a stranger in the area with essentially no market. The best qualities I had going for me, as I look back, were reasonable intelligence and a high degree of motivation. However, when I made the commitment to stay in the business that Sunday afternoon, it was my faith that gave me the strength and courage to do it.

My maternal grandfather was a Methodist minister and I am his namesake. My mother always had a modest hope as I was growing up that I might follow in his footsteps. The "call" to take that step never came, but primarily because of her teaching and example I have always had a strong religious base in my life for which I am most grateful.

There are many ways to make money—even lots of money—which did not interest me then and still do not. The more I thought about it the more I realized that the insurance business would provide me what I wanted out of life—an opportunity to enjoy an above average income and at the same time make a significant contribution in the lives of other people. Furthermore, my work schedule would be sufficiently flexible that I could live my faith as a dedicated layman in my church. I found this very appealing and I have always felt that somehow the Lord led me to make insurance my life's work. I am happy to say that my mother learned to accept my decision and was proud of me and the success I enjoyed.

Although my religious faith and my desire to have a career compatible with that faith were at the heart of the decision I made that Sunday afternoon, my faith in the support and encouragement I could expect from my wife, Grace, also was a very positive influence. She was a real asset then and continues to be. The faith I had in my associates and my company were also supportive and I was prepared to put forth whatever was necessary in work and study to justify everyone's faith in me.

I found I could develop more confidence and faith in myself by comparing myself with established insurance people I met. When I got to know them I discovered that, in the words of the old saw, they "put their pants on one leg at a time" just as I did. I concluded that if I applied myself to the utmost of my ability there was no reason I could not be as successful as they were. The results have greatly exceeded my expectations.

I have related this personal story in some detail to demonstrate how important the three kinds of faith have been in my life. I believe they are all necessary if we are to reach our full potential as human beings and as business people. Each is gained or lost a little bit at a time. Furthermore, faith—all three kinds—is a personal matter. Each of us has to work at it in his or her own way. The extent to which you do not have all three is a limitation on your ability. It is one you can do something about if you choose to do so—but you must work at it like everything else. And you do it one step at a time.

Faith in yourself is an absolute must for personal growth and accomplishment. And your faith in yourself can be increased immeasurably by an active religious faith and a healthy faith in other people. All of us can do far more than we have ever done. But it takes faith to recognize this and to do something about it.

A number of years ago one of the speakers at the GAMC LAMP Meeting was a gentleman by the name of Dr. Tom Haggai. All I recall about his background was that he was a Lebanese by nationality and a Baptist minister by profession.

I will never forget, however, the prayer he told us he prayed every morning. It goes like this: "Dear Lord, don't let me die until I am dead."

I think that is a great prayer for every one of us—no matter what our age. Life is for living and we have the opportunity—particularly in this business—to live all the way out! Yes, you can increase your faith by working at it—and the extent to which you do not is a self-imposed limitation.

WHAT WE GIVE

Finally, a sixth limitation is in *what we give from what the Lord has so generously given to us.*

I sometimes wonder if we really appreciate how fortunate we are to live in the United States of America. Grace and I have travelled a great deal including such out of the way countries as India and Mainland China. The standard of living we have in this country is totally incomprehensible to people in those two countries—and for that matter most areas in the world. Yet, we have a tendency, sometimes, to take it for granted.

Most of us are American citizens—and we accept the fact we are without appreciating the privileges and benefits that go with American citizenship. Our oldest daugher, Nancy, while attending the University of Washington, became friends with a married couple from Hong Kong who were also attending the University. After graduation when their visas had expired they moved back to Hong Kong. When their first child arrived the father remained at his job in Hong Kong, and when it came time for the baby to be delivered the mother contrived to be admitted to a hospital in Bellingham, Washington, so that the baby would be a U.S. citizen. That was how much she valued something that all of us tend to take for granted.

Not only do we have the privilege of living in this great country but most of the readers of this book are fortunate to be in the life insurance business. Ours is an unlimited opportunity for income and personal satisfaction by providing a unique and extremely valuable service to others. After 38 years, as far as I am concerned, this is still the greatest business in the world.

Because we are so fortunate, I think it is important that we ask ourselves what we are giving back to the business and to the community and country in which we live. Some who read this are undoubtedly giving a great deal. Others probably should be doing more. There may be some who are giving back absolutely nothing.

In 1971, Grace and I stood on the beach of the Dead Sea. It is not an attractive body of water—either to the eye or to the nose. I'm sure you all know why it is so unattractive. The reason, of course, is that it has an inlet but no outlet. It takes but it doesn't give.

I've known some people like that. Perhaps you have too. Please do not misunderstand me. I am not suggesting that I have all the answers or that I have done it all. But I continue to follow Jonathan Livingston Seagull's advice to overcome my limitations in order—patiently!

I think that is a sound goal for each of us. Furthermore, medical authorities are in agreement that it is therapeutic to give of ourselves without any specific thought of return. But I guarantee that what you give of yourself in time, money and effort in church, synagogue, community and industry affairs will come back to you 100 fold in various ways. This has been my personal experience.

To give is to grow as a human being—and there is no limit to what each of us can give and grow except those that are self-imposed!

I have been discussing the "infinities of life."

1. There is no limit to what people can do—
work, effort.

2. There is no limit to what people can know—
knowledge, skill.

3. There is no limit to what people can be—
attitude, faith.

4. And there is no limit to what people can give of themselves of what the Lord has given to them—except those limitations which are self-imposed.

We only go through this life once—no second chances, no instant replays. And only we, as individuals, can decide what we will make of our opportunities. The world is full of what I call "gonna-guys" and "gonna-gals." They are always "gonna" do this and they are "gonna" do that. They make all kinds of promises to themselves and to other people —and nothing happens! If you fall in that category I would encourage you to make some changes. You will never regret it and you will find your life much more meaningful and rewarding in every way.

* * *

7.

WHAT KIND OF AGENCY?

There are many different kinds of very successful life insurance agencies. Furthermore, many established agencies currently are in the process of making significant changes in the way they operate and just about every agency head for one reason or another, is seriously evaluating where his or her agency is as compared to where they want it to be. This is not a totally new phenomenon. Successful agency managers have always analyzed their agency operations, particularly at year-end, with the hope of finding ways to make them more productive and more profitable. However, the extent and the rapidity of the changes taking place currently is new and somewhat bewildering even to the most experienced life insurance executive.

In addition to the self-appraisal which is an integral part of the manager's business life, the home office has begun to take an even more direct hand in his planning. Company management has had to bite the bullet on costs, and their once benign view of how a manager might handle his agency affairs has given way to an "our-way-or-else" attitude within which the manager must seek his way. Today's company can no longer afford the luxury of encouraging off-beat attitudes or methods.

In order that all of us are on the same wavelength, let me define our areas of consideration. We will only be discussing so-called ordinary agencies. Home service agencies and "debit agencies" are also experiencing change but my personal knowledge of those operations is so limited that it is better not to bring them into this discussion. The kinds of agencies that we will consider might be described as follows: first, multiline; second, "general practitioner"; third, advanced marketing; and fourth, sophisticated.

Let me describe what kind of agency, in my opinion, tends to fit into each cateogory:

A multiline agency generally sells all kinds of personal coverages, plus all forms of property and casualty insurance. Although the other types of agencies may sell these same products, their marketing approach and agency structure are entirely different. In a true multiline agency, property and casualty is used as the basic prospecting tool. Other products are then sold to P and C customers, with the goal of having all of a policyholder's insurance needs handled by the one company. This type of agency does its business for the most part in the broad middle income market and the agents are not permitted to broker business with other companies.

The "general practitioner" type of agency places its emphasis on the sale of life insurance primarily for family security needs. A fair number of business insurance and basic estate planning sales will be made in this agency and even some P and C will be sold by certain agents to their policyholders. However, this business in some instances will be placed outside the life company which may not have P and C in its portfolio—although the number of these grows smaller daily. Other products will be sold in varying amounts—disability pay, health insurance, small and large group, pensions, etc.—and placed with those companies which have the products and brokered by the agents whose companies do not. Basic computer backup services for such things as sales illustrations will be available at low cost to the agents. Many times an agency of this type will represent a company which does not have the products to compete successfully in the advanced market field.

An advanced marketing agency does most of its business in the business insurance and estate planning fields. New agents are recruited and trained to move into those markets at the outset of their careers. Adequate computer backup services are available to service this market at modest cost to the agents. A pension company may be part of the agency. The company offers a broad range of products designed to penetrate these target markets. An attorney quite often may be housed in the agency to work with the agents. A considerable amount of business is done with nonlife products—annuities, disability pay, group insurance, pensions, tax-shelters, etc. Property and casualty quite often will be handled by a separate department. In fact, in many such agencies there may be a number of departments, each of which is responsible for one type of business. The agency does most of its business in the upper income markets.

The sophisticated agency is designed to be in the "financial planning" market. The goal is for the agents to work with "peak" prospects insofar as income is concerned. The latest and most sophisticated in backup services are available. Less than 50% of the commissions paid are on life insurance sales. Fees are becoming an increasing source of income. Tax shelters of all kinds are part of the product mix and much of the business will be placed outside the principal company. An attorney and probably a CPA are on the agency's staff; perhaps even experts in certain investment devices. High earnings per agent are realized and the agency's recruiting is targeted toward the type of agent who can move quickly into this field. Agents limit their activities to a relatively few clients for whom they give superior service in all the financial planning areas and as a result substantial sales are made, using the full gamut of financial products. Specialized training and field supervision is available from highly qualified and well paid staff people.

These descriptions of the various types of agencies are by no means complete. However, I believe they do provide a basis for a manager to get a pretty good idea of what type of agency he currently has plus some ideas of what will be required to become a different type of agency.

FIVE POINTS TO CONSIDER

There are five basic points for a manager to consider as he contemplates what kind of agency he wants ultimately to build:

The first (and probably the most important) *is what kind of company does the manager represent and what is its marketing philosophy?* How would you judge the leadership in the home office? Are they committed to lead the company in the direction you are considering and give you the support and back up you will need? How about the underwriting? Is it compatible with the markets you wish to penetrate? What is your company's attitude toward brokerage business in the agency? How much flexibility do you have in assigning staff responsibilities and determining the amount and basis for their compensation? What can you expect your company to *do,* based on past performance, as contrasted with what they say they *are going to do?* This is a very key question.

I am sure you can think of additional questions to which the manager will want satisfactory answers if he is considering making a major change. However, these offer a reasonably good start.

The second consideration is products. Will the company's portfolio enable the agency to compete favorably in the markets in which the manager wants to operate? If the products are not now in the ratebook, when can they be expected? Can the manager count on the product line being updated on an ongoing basis in order that the agency can not only be competitive currently, but also stay that way? Will the company allow the manager to control and be compensated for the brokering by the agents in the agency of those products which are not available or are totally noncompetitive with other companies?

Parenthetically, let me add that there has been considerable contraction in the time between when the field demands a new product and the company is ready to offer it. Traditionally, this might have been a matter of years; with sophisticated computer techniques, it can now be a matter of weeks.

A third consideration is the qualifications of the people presently associated with the manager. If, as a group, they have considerable expertise in the advanced marketing fields, there would appear to be a solid base for "upgrading" the agency. This would be particularly true if among the group were some qualified staff people capable of attracting additional agents whom they can train and supervise to work in the more advanced markets.

A fourth consideration is the location of the agency. Although I know there are exceptions, logic indicates that a metropolitan area is a better spot in which to operate an advanced marketing or sophisticated agency than a small town or rural area. Generally speaking, the larger population will provide more of the higher income prospects—corporations and other businesses of all kinds plus more professional people—than would be found in smaller communities. In addition, chances are there will be more prospective recruits from which to select, with the education and background characteristics desired, in a larger city.

The final consideration is the manager himself. Where is he coming from? Does he have the commitment, ability and financial wherewithal to manage a different type of agency? Does he have the staff or the demonstrated ability to attract, train and develop the assistants that he must have to get the job done? Is he mentally and emotionally prepared to pay the price in work and worry that will be required? Does he have the organizational and administrative skills that will be required? Is it possible that he has already reached his "highest level of competence" and is just asking for trouble?

It should be mentioned that once a manager has put into action his plans to upgrade, the genie is usually out of the bottle and he will find it extremely difficult to backtrack. That is the prime reason why his plans for upgrading should be fully conceived before he makes his move.

Let's apply these five considerations to a hypothetical agency from each of our four groups and see how the manager might use them to make the best possible decision.

MULTILINE TO GENERAL PRACTITIONER

First of all, let's consider a typical multiline agency whose manager would like to operate more like a "general practitioner" type of agency. It is obvious that in order to do so he will have to sell his home office on permitting him to deviate significantly from his company's marketing philosophy. He would need an outstanding record to have any chance of making that sale. In addition he would probably feel he needed some different products, although his present portfolio is ideally suited for his present type of operation. His company would probably point out that it is doing very well operating as it is and that it isn't about to change for one manager.

After giving it some further thought the agency head might conclude that it would make good sense for him to set a goal of becoming the most successful manager in his company. If, on the other hand, this career path does not appeal to him, he has two choices: either make the necessary adjustment so that he can be happy where he is or seek an opportunity with a company which will give him a chance someday to manage one of the other three types of agencies we have described above.

I know a manager of a multiline agency who presently is faced with making precisely the type of decision I have described above. This particular manager is quite knowledgeable in the advanced marketing fields. He would like to build an agency of full-time special agents doing a fair amount of their production in the business insurance and estate planning fields. He is capable of producing personally in these fields and has demonstrated the ability to attract new agents who can produce in the markets. However, the product line and backup service he has to work with are not designed to penetrate these markets and it is surprising that he is doing as well as he is. He has the same two choices that I described for the manager of the hypothetical multiline agency if he wants to remain in management, for there is no chance that his company will change. They are doing too well with their present operation.

"GENERAL PRACTITIONER" TO ADVANCED MARKETING

Let us now consider a "general practitioner" type of agency whose manager would like to have it become an advanced marketing agency. This transition is more feasible than the one we have just discussed. Furthermore, it can be a gradual change without greatly disturbing the present operation. The first thing for the manager to do is analyze his present organization. How much of his agency's production is coming from the advanced markets at the present time? How many of his associates are qualified to operate effectively in these markets? How about his product line—is it adequate and sufficiently competitive for him to make the change? Will his company be responsive over a period of time to giving him the products he needs which he does not presently have? Does he have the confidence and respect of the company officers to the point that they will react favorably and have a personal interest in helping him?

If he is encouraged by the answers to these questions, and makes the decision to go ahead, the manager's first challenge is to upgrade his present organization. His first attention should be to his supervisory staff. Those who are not CLUs should be required to enroll and obtain the designation without delay. Those who are already CLUs should be encouraged to qualify for the new designation, Chartered Financial Consultant. Those who have not completed business and estate planning courses should be required to fit them into their development program. In other words, the manager must make certain that his staff people are knowledgeable in these fields and capable of training others. Of course, the manager himself should have previously touched all of these bases so that he is able to lead by example.

The manager's next move is to select his best qualified associates and together with his supervisors, concentrate on moving them totally into the advanced markets. It goes without saying that these agents must be provided with adequate computer backup service. Hopefully, the company will at least share in the cost. If this is not available, the manager must make the capital investment and sell his associates on sharing in the ongoing usage and maintenance costs.

Specialized training classes with or without company support will have to be conducted regularly and, at first, limited to those agents with sufficient expertise to profit from their attendance, and contribute on a positive basis to the discussions. The formation of one or more study groups within the agency or, perhaps, with some members of other agencies, within or outside the agent's principal company, should be encouraged.

Joint field work should be actively promoted. This can be effective in many ways. Agents who are now reasonably qualified and are included in the special training classes will be inclined to make more calls in the advanced markets with an associate than they will on their own. Furthermore, teaming a well qualified agent with a new and/or less knowledgeable associate is an ideal way to expose the neophyte to the market and get him or her excited about its potential. The prospects he can provide for the senior agent are a plus for him and so the arrangement can be mutually profitable. Considerable emphasis must also be given to changing prospecting habits throughout the agency but particularly with those agents who have been selected as the best qualified to lead during the initial transition period. The goal for them is to be doing *all* of their prospecting in the business insurance and estate planning fields and the sooner this occurs, without adversely affecting current production, the better.

Selection standards for new recruits will probably have to be raised. A college education, as a minimum, should be required with a major in business, finance, or accounting preferred. Most new agents, however, should have been out of college for a few years and had some practical business experience. Only the brightest and highly motivated young college graduates should be considered and it might be desirable to have them work inside the agency in some sort of trainee position before introducing them to the agent's job as a possible career. Obviously, the manager must be prepared to finance new associates at high amounts as the people he wants and needs will also be attractive to other employers.

All of this activity is fairly basic. However, if it is carried on consistently over a period of time, the agency climate will change, new agents will be more easily led into the more advanced markets early in their careers, and the agency will be on its way to making the transition the manager wants with relatively modest disruption.

There are some downside risks, however, which must be anticipated and evaluated before putting his plan into operation. First of all, when agents become more knowledgeable and are working and studying in these fields they become more acutely aware of any inadequacies or shortcomings which may exist in their company's product line. For various reasons, there will be a tendency for agents to place more and more business with other companies. They will do this for what they feel are totally justifiable reasons which the manager will have difficulty refuting. The manager or general agent may be placed in an untenable position unless he does something. He may find it unprofitable to pay the rent, clerical, telephone, and other costs for an agency force which is putting a substantial portion of its business with other companies.

There are several ways to attack this problem—some better than others. The best way is for the manager to convince his company of the necessity of providing the field with a sufficiently broad and competitive portfolio so that his associates will put the lion's share of their business through the agency. If this cannot be done, the agency head will want to consider making arrangements with certain companies that can provide the products his associates need and will pay him an override. He can then either sell his agents on using this facility or require them to do so. Hopefully, his company will permit him to do this. To a certain extent the same situation can be managed, particularly with high-producing agents, by giving them allowances for office space, secretarial, telephone, etc., on the basis of first-year commissions paid for with the agency's principal company or the brokerage facility which the manager is controlling, and requiring them to pay their own expenses.

Another risk to anticipate is the demand for more and more in the way of backup support. The need for a pension company with all the headaches and expense that entails is almost certain to come up. The manager will certainly want to move slowly before he makes this commitment of money and headaches. He may want to consider using an outside service. But this brings the risk of having his agents attracted to another agency or organization which will provide something for them which he is unwilling to do. Some managers and general agents feel it is their responsibility to provide, within reason, everything their agents need to operate in the advanced markets in order to justify their loyalty and business.

The costs and risks can be substantial and the manager may want to "make haste slowly" as he contemplates all the factors to be considered.

The need for an expanding and competent staff will be vital. An attorney will be invaluable as the agency becomes involved in more complicated cases. Getting the attorney licensed and having him share commissions on certain cases may be the answer on a temporary basis. However, it is unlikely this will work out over a sustained period. Chances are there will come a time when the agency will have to assume this expense, just as it does for other members of staff.

There are undoubtedly other considerations and potential problems which I have not included and which may occur to the manager who is considering making this transition in his agency. Suffice it to say that it is not an easy change to make and it will take a number of years to bring it about. Furthermore, as has been indicated, it probably will require a substantial investment of capital. Hopefully, if all goes well, the manager will make it all back eventually with considerable profit. But it is important to realize that there are risks. In addition, it will require a great amount of effort by the manager. As you decide what to do you might consider what was said many years ago about those who joined the Lewis and Clark Expedition to the West Coast: "The cowards never started and the weak ones fell by the way."

THE SOPHISTICATED AGENCY

Let us now consider the manager of an advanced marketing agency who wants to change it into a sophisticated agency. Many of the same steps I have just outlined will have to be taken, depending, of course, on the current status of the agency. It would seem that only a well established and very successful advanced marketing agency should consider making this change. And for this type of agency the transition might not be too difficult.

There probably will be a need for more products, particularly for tax shelters and specialized tax planning. Probably the agency should be more departmentalized with vice presidents or their equivalents heading up each. The departments can be broken down by product or function or a combination of both. The marketing thrust of the agency will be financial planning on a very broad basis. The specific differences between an avdanced marketing agency and a sophisticated agency will probably fall in the following general areas:

The sophisticated agency will strive to serve a higher income type of prospect. It will have a broader portfolio of products to offer. A higher percentage of commissions will be paid on nonlife products and more business placed with other companies as compared with the business placed with the agency's principal company. More of the people in the agency will have the Chartered Financial Consultant or Certified Financial Planner designation and more sophisticated computer back-up of all kinds will be available. The sophisticated agency will probably have more highly qualified professionals on its staff including a tax attorney and a CPA. There will probably be less commitment to the life insurance product in the traditional way and more emphasis on satisfying the needs and desires of the discriminating prospect for financial products and services of all kinds. There will be more income coming to members of the sophisticated agency from fees.

The entire matter of fee-for-service compensation is too confused in the mid-'80s for clear discussion. It seems to me unlikely that clients will pay fees where the seller gets adequate commission compensation. In other areas, fees will probably become more common over time.

These are just a few of the differences. Others will become apparent as the manager of an advanced marketing agency considers making the change. It will be obvious that a further capital investment will have to be made, and the question answered—will it be worth it? The manager also will have to decide if he, too, may not have reached his "highest level of competence" and that it would be a mistake for him to let his ego lead him down the primrose path.

I have tried in this chapter to give the reader a bird's-eye view of four different kinds of career agent agencies. I have not discussed brokerage as part of an agency's production. The typical multiline company neither accepts brokerage business nor permits its agents to place business with other companies. Some agencies of the other three types represent companies which accept brokerage and some do not. Obviously, it will be a factor to consider as a manager contemplates building his present agency or making a decision to upgrade his organization. Each situation will be different. There is a tendency, however, for brokers to be fickle. They are not a reliable source of business year in and year out and should be looked upon as plus business to help pay the costs of building an agency of career agents.

I recognize that the managers who read this chapter will represent many different companies and be in various stages in the building of their agencies. Furthermore, it is interesting to know that despite all the discussion on the platform and in the media regarding the great movement by the life insurance business into the financial planning field, according to LIMRA figures only 10% of the life insurance sold in 1982 was placed in companies whose marketing philosophy is recognized by the industry as being geared toward the advanced marketing and sophisticated fields.

Obviously, there are isolated agencies with other companies which are very successful penetrating these markets, and not all of the agencies in the companies whose goal is to secure its business in the peak market are actually doing it. However, these figures would seem to indicate that a high percentage of the business is still being produced by multiline and general practitioner type of agencies.

Whatever kind of agency you have, the most important thing is to be happy and successful. Do not be concerned with what someone else is doing or contemplating doing. As I write elsewhere in this book—if your home office is satisfied, if your spouse is satisfied and if you are reasonably satisfied, you are successful. And that is what it is all about.

* * *

8.

RIGHT OR LEFT AT OAK STREET

This title provides me with considerable latitide which can be desirable on occasion, as one's concepts do change dramatically as circumstances change. And "circumstances" are changing in the insurance business almost daily.

As I thought about the title I was reminded of the story about the young unmarried child psychologist who had just graduated from college. He was asked to make a speech to a group of parents, most of whom had teenagers. He chose as his title, "Ten Rules on the Raising of Children." Later on he married and had three small children. When asked to make a speech to a similar audience he then chose, "Ten Suggestions on the Raising of Children." More years passed and by then he had five children, and one a teenager. Again he was asked to speak to a similar audience and he chose as his title, "Ten Helpful Hints on the Raising of Children." Later when he had four teenagers and one aged 12 he was asked to speak to the same kind of group. This time he chose as his title, "Crisis in the Communication Process."

My purpose here is to communicate some serious thoughts on a subject life insurance people are concerned with every working day—as it relates to other people! The subject is "growing older." No one likes the idea of growing old but as you have heard said many times, "It's a lot better than the alternative."

There is a little poem which expresses some thoughts with which I think all of us can identify. I don't know who the author is, but it goes like this:

> When as a child, I laughed and wept,
>   Time crept.
> When as a youth, I dreamed and talked,
>   Time walked.
> When I became a full grown man,
>   Time ran.
> And later, as I older grew,
>   Time flew.
> Soon I shall find while travelling on,
>   Time gone.

Every time I read that verse or think about it, I am struck with its validity. The four years I was in high school lasted a long time. The 6½ years I was in the U.S. Navy lasted forever. The 30 years I managed an agency was a significant part of my life. However, each of the last 10 years seemed to pass so much more quickly than did those earlier years. And I find it very difficult to believe that my retirement from Prudential began in late '82. It has gone by so quickly.

Most of you are doubtless feeling the increasing rapidity with which time is passing. It is a sobering thought and although not a particularly happy one, it is not a situation we can ignore. I don't consider myself an expert on the subject of growing older, but I do have some ideas which I hope you will find interesting.

As I see it, the basic desire of most of us is to have a healthy, happy and productive life throughout our working career. I don't believe anyone would disagree with this objective. Healthy, happy, productive—each word connotes many needs and desires. In the years remaining for each of us it would seem desirable that we continue from where we are with that goal in mind.

Unfortunately, it has been my observation that too many people do not realize these basic desires or at least not as fully as they might like. I think I have a little insight into why this is so which I have gleaned from observation, plus the writings and speeches of people more qualified than I.

A song which caught my ear several years ago was country-western singer Roy Clark's recording of "Right or Left at Oak Street." It tells about a commuter from suburbia, who is bored and frustrated with his way of life and contemplates just running away from it all. The closing line of the lyric goes like this: "Right or left at Oak Street, it's the choice I make every day. And I don't know which takes more courage, the stayin' or the runnin' away."

I suspect that many of the readers of this book, if they were completely honest, would have to admit that at least occasionally they have or have had similar thoughts cross their mind. In most instances these thoughts probably aren't serious and they are forgotten almost immediately. But the fact that they do occur cannot be ignored, so perhaps we should contemplate why they occur and what can be done about them.

Several years ago I became fascinated by two books which seem to offer some explanation of why people become bored and frustrated as well as how they can learn to live more healthy, happy and productive lives.

The first book was on the best-seller list for many weeks and has been widely quoted. I am sure you are familiar with it. It is called *The Peter Principle,* by Dr. Lawrence Peter and Raymond Hull. Dr. Peter's principle as explained by the co-author, Raymond Hull, is this: in any hierarchy, be it corporation, university, or military establishment, people tend to rise to their "highest level of incompetence." In other words, the really competent people at every level are promoted and the incompetent ones remain. As a result, most organizations tend to be run by people who are incompetent at their present level of responsibility.

Granted it is a "tongue-in-cheek" concept, but it does touch some sensitive areas. We have all seen it in our business —highly competent people are promoted to positions in management, both in the field and the home office, for which they are relatively incompetent. Or certainly not as competent as they were in their former positions. And they probably are not nearly as healthy and happy as they were and perhaps could be again in their old spots.

In some ways you would have to call *The Peter Principle* a negative book and I don't like to think about or discuss negative ideas. But if by any chance you haven't read it, or if you would like to refresh your memory, you might be able to find or borrow a copy. It will give you something to think about and may help you understand some of the frustration and boredom you have observed.

The other book is called, *How To Get What You Want* and its author is also Raymond Hull. (Incidentally, Mr. Hull makes his home in Vancouver, B.C. and my wife, Grace, who also is a writer, and I have met him on a couple of occasions.) This book never made the best-seller lists and the chances are that very few of you will have even so much as heard of it before. But it is jam packed with specific, constructive and positive procedures on how to get what you want. I don't know whether it is still in print. It was published by Funk and Wagnalls, if you would like to get a copy. I recommend it.

One of the reasons I like the book so much, I'm sure, is because I agree with just about every idea in it. And so may you. Mr. Hull lays it out in a manner which challenges the reader to do something specific. He states categorically that you don't have to have faith in him; you don't have to believe him; but if you do what he says to do, the results will surprise and please you. I can say that I followed his instructions and it has worked in my life.

The difficulty with too many people is that they have not taken the time or made the effort to decide what they really want. Too often they are influenced by what other people feel they should want, or what other people have, or what custom seems to dictate they should want. Outside influences take over and before they know it they may be trying "to keep up with the Joneses." Or they may permit themselves to fall into a rut and they can't see any way to get out of it.

People who have worked with me through the years have heard me say repeatedly, "Be careful what you ask for because you may get it." Too often people spend their lives working for something and, when they are successful, they find it isn't what they want at all. It is difficult to be healthy, happy, and productive under those circumstances.

A specific example of this is someone I know very well. From the beginning of his insurance career this individual wanted to be a vice president. Starting as an agent, he touched all the bases—very successful at personal selling, excellent supervisor and outstanding manager of a substantial agency. He was very competent at managing an agency and undoubtedly would have built one of the super agencies for his company. However, he still had this thing about being a vice president. I guess you would have to say it was a matter of ego. He somehow felt that to realize his potential he had to have the fancy title and the prestige that goes with it. So he started up the home office ladder.

It would be charitable to say that home office work at the vice presidential level was out of his comfort zone. It was simply a perfect example of the Peter Principle in real life. By the time it became apparent to everyone, including him, that he was not cut out for the job, his age was such that neither he nor the home office thought it made sense for him to return to the field as an agency manager. Consequently, he elected to take early retirement. I can't help feeling there must be times when he thinks of "what might have been."

I'm sure that at the heart of his desire to be a vice president was the feeling that he would then be more successful than by just being a manager. I have never felt that way. Through the years I had several opportunities to become a vice president with Prudential and to have even fancier titles with other companies. It never was particularly difficult for me to say, "Thanks, but no thanks," to those offers. I always felt that, for me, managing a life insurance agency was the greatest job in the world. And I have no regrets; I still feel that way.

A fairly significant number of unhappy people have difficulty serving permanently in a role in which they perceive themselves as playing "second fiddle." Realistically, however, most of us will spend the greater part, if not all, of our lives in that role. No matter how phenomenally we succeed, or how high we rise in the company, or how much wealth we accumulate, or how respected we become, there will always be people ahead of us. Those of us who find ourselves in that situation may do well to accept the fact that only a few can play first fiddle. Even among equals, someone must have the responsibility of making the final decision. While there may be five licensed drivers in the automobile, there is room for only one behind the steering wheel.

It is important that we learn to accept ourselves for what we are. We should recognize our strong points and use them to the fullest. In the final analysis, what is important is how well we do at any task *in comparison to our abilities.* One reason I think golf is such a great lifetime game is the handicap system. It enables two golfers with established handicaps to enjoy a competitive round of golf, even though one is age 45 with a 10 handicap and the other age 75 with a 25 handicap. Personally, I play golf with people of many ages—from

25 to 81—on a fairly regular basis and I enjoy them all. If we can accept the fact in our personal lives, as we do on the golf course, that, for whatever reason, people do not have comparable abilities, we will have taken a giant step toward finding that healthy, happy and productive life-style we all want.

Here are some specific suggestions which have been helpful to me through the years:

- As Mr. Hull states in his book *How To Get What You Want,* the first thing to do is write down what you really want out of the remainder of your life. I cannot emphasize too much how important this is. Obviously, people from different age groups will have significantly different items on their lists. The important thing is that it be *your* list. Don't be influenced by what others might say or think as you are writing. And don't show it to anyone—even your spouse! Undoubtedly you will discuss certain items with her or him as you are preparing the list. But when you have it completed, keep it to yourself. As Mr. Hull points out, if you don't plan on other people seeing it, you can and will be far more personal. You don't have to impress anyone or have any feeling of embarrassment. There is an excellent chance, if you make a conscientious effort, that this list will come very close to being exactly what you want.

- High on the list will have to be a better than average income. Do not minimize that need. You probably cannot think in terms of making less money—or doing less business—but perhaps you can put your business activities in a different perspective with other objectives. Maybe you can figure how to run your agency, instead of letting it run you. Tied in with this, and high on your list, might be a better relationship with your spouse and family.

- Make a contribution in the lives of other people other than what you already do by being in the life insurance business. You are probably deeply involved in outside activities of various kinds. But perhaps you may want to reexamine the motives for what you are doing. It is therapeutic in many ways to give time and money with no strings attached.

- Be determined to work at your health—regular exercise, relaxation, annual physical exams—you have heard it all many times. But what are you doing about it? I know many people who talk about doing these things, particularly regular exercise, and then they do little or nothing about it. An hour a day swimming, walking, jogging, etc., will do wonders for your health. Put it on your list and do it! And how about cigarette smoking? Just recently I read the newest statistics. About 75% to 80% of *all* lung cancer cases are found among cigarette smokers and the risk of developing lung cancer is 10 times greater for smokers than nonsmokers. If you are still smoking, this is a great suggestion for your list. Bear in mind that you will have a much better chance of having good health if you work at it than you will if you don't!

I won't make any further attempts to add to your list. This is a personal matter. But keep this in mind—you *currently* have a list of things you are working for, but perhaps the list has come about by *default* rather than by *design*. Most important of all, the things you are working for may not be what you really want, if you will only take the time and make the effort to decide what your goals should be to achieve that healthy, happy, productive life.

Nowhere do I mean that we shouldn't have high goals. The industry needs leaders in the home offices and the field as well as in its professional organizations. Rather, we should attempt to balance our lives and keep everything in perspective. It has been said many times that there isn't much point in becoming the richest person in the cemetery. I hope you would agree as you plan your future.

Years ago I ran across an old fable. I have no idea where it came from or who wrote it, but I think it makes as strong a case for establishing priorities as I have ever seen. It goes like this:

"There was a wise old king who was nearing the end of his reign. His days being numbered, he was concerned as to which of his three sons would succeed him on the throne. One day he called the three boys before him. 'My sons,' he said, 'I am old and must soon drop the reins of power. Unto one of you will fall the mantle of sovereignty. Last night I had a dream. Give me your answer to my dream, and I shall tell you which one shall be the king after me.'

" 'In my dream we set out to hunt the golden falcon, the most coveted prize in the realm. With our servants we rode into the deep forest in search of the giant bird. Farther and farther we rode, past the great dam which held back the river, until at last in the evening we came upon a clearing, lush with heavy grass, which ended at the brink of a steep precipice. At the foot of the gorge lay a village, just settling to sleep. There, high on the limb of a tall tree on the opposite side of the clearing, we suddenly beheld the golden falcon, his feathers gleaming in the twilight. Hastily we dismounted, drawing our bows, each eager to be the first to claim the prize sought by all the huntsmen in the land.

" 'But as we fixed the arrow on the string, suddenly the heavens darkened. The thunder rolled and the lightning flashed. The earth shook as, with a mighty roar, the great dam burst, sending its torrent of angry water headlong over the precipice, straight toward the sleeping village. The lightning struck, and one of our servants was hurled, bleeding and unconscious to the ground. Now, my sons, in such a situation what would you do?'

" 'My father,' said the eldest son, 'the first concern of a king should be for the welfare of his people. The faithful servant lies bleeding and hurt on the ground. Surely the first concern should be for him. I would give him aid, binding his wounds, and administering treatment to bring him back to consciousness, and make him comfortable for the journey home.'

" 'Truly, my son, a monarch should be merciful. The servant, indeed, deserves attention. That is a good answer.'

"Then he turned to the second son. 'And what,' he asked, 'would you do?'

" 'A king should indeed be merciful. But, my father, the great dam has burst. Below are many people asleep, unaware of the danger which approaches. I believe that the lives of many are of greater importance than the welfare of one servant. Therefore, I would immediately fly to the village, awaken the people and urge them to flee to the high hills and safety.'

" 'A fit ruler should indeed be concerned with the safety of his people,' said the king. 'You show yourself to have that concern. You have made a good answer.'

"Finally he turned to his youngest son. 'What would you do if this situation confronted you?' he asked.

" 'My father,' said the youngest son, 'I would keep my eye on the spot where the wing meets the body and would slowly draw the bow taut for the kill!'

" 'And you, my son, shall inherit my kingdom,' said the king, 'for you have shown yourself to possess the rare ability to keep your eye on the main goal. You will not allow yourself to be led astray by unessentials, important in themselves, but not vital to the main objective before you! You shall succeed me on the throne!' "

I am sure that some who read this will question the king's decision. They may well be people who do not recognize the importance of having well-defined priorities in their own lives. Bear in mind that in our example the chance to kill the golden falcon was fleeting. It was now or never. The leader in this incident, if it were a true story, could kill the falcon and then almost immediately tend to the servant and send someone to warn the sleeping village. In other words, all three situations could have been handled expeditiously by a king who understood priorities and could make quick decisions.

The moral in this story can be applied in preparing the list of what you want to do with your life from now on. Do not underestimate what you are capable of doing as the first two sons did in the fable. Make certain your priorities are in order, however, in order that you will do first things first.

It is important to understand and accept, however, that no matter how well we plan our lives and establish our priorities, misfortune may come our way. It is at that time that our faith will be put to the test of sustaining us. Recognizing that this could happen, it behooves all of us to include in our list of activities attendance and participation in the church of our choice.

* * *

9.

POST-MORTEMS AND SECOND CHANCES

Sports fans are prone to engage in post-mortems on a fairly regular basis. At baseball games they always know what the manager should have done. For example, if the manager has the batter hit away with a runner on first and no one out and he grounds into a doubleplay, the fans know he *should have* had the batter sacrifice the runner into scoring position. This is particularly true if the next batter laces a long single into right field which would have easily scored a runner from second. Or how about the football coach who has his team go for the touchdown on fourth down from the one yard line early in the game—and comes up empty. When his team loses the game by two points, the fans all know he *should have* kicked the field goal. And then there is the professional golfer who tries to hit his second shot on a par five hole over the water in front of the green—and does not quite make it. The result is a bogie six. When he loses the tournament and the $100,000 first place money by one stroke he might wish he had played more conservatively and laid up to the water.

Aside from the obvious medical definition, a true post-mortem is not a critical one-sided opinion. Rather it is an examination where all the possibilities and factors should be considered before a judgment is rendered. In the baseball example one should not ignore the fact that at the time the manager made the decision for the batter to hit away, his club may have been behind by several runs, and it made good sense for him to play for a big inning. In the football example, one should not ignore the fact that seven points early in the game means much more than three insofar as momentum and game plan are concerned. And as for the golfer, if he had reached the green and made an eagle, the momentum would have swung his way and, who knows, he might have won the tournament going away.

This chapter will be a post-mortem and not a one-sided opinion on my 30 years as Prudential's manager in Seattle. It will be written in the first person as I describe some of the mistakes I made, my rationalizations for having made them, and what I would strive to do if I had a second chance. Perhaps you, as a reader, will be able to identify with some of these mistakes and learn from them while you are still in a position to do so.

CONTRACTING PROBLEMS

One mistake I made over and over again was to contract with agents whose qualifications I knew were marginal. Every time I did I swore I wouldn't be guilty of doing it again (as I paid the financing loss). But I always was, even up to my last few months on the job.

In retrospect I can understand why I continued to make this same mistake—but I cannot justify my doing it. Let me explain what I mean by that somewhat ambiguous statement. First of all may I point out that these so-called marginal candidates that I persisted in hiring through the years were not "dogs." In each instance the prospective agent had passed the LIMRA test with a score of 12 or better. They had scored reasonably well on a mental agility test that we used in Prudential and they had passed a physical examination.

But in each instance, as I look back, there were one or more glaring weaknesses which, for some inexplicable reason, I chose to ignore. For example, many of them were too young and immature. I had myself convinced that maturity is not measured by the calendar, and to a certain extent I still believe that is true. But somehow I invariably felt that the 22- or 23-year-old I was currently evaluating was *mature beyond his years* and was a good candidate for success in our business. He had done well on the tests, his market was fair, if not strong, he had a good education and he had done reasonably well in precontract study and selling. Why, then, did I have no survivors in my agency when I retired who were younger than 25 years at the time I brought them under contract—and we recruited a goodly number?

I suppose it could be said that we didn't know how to work with them. To me that sounds like a home office generalization, although in some instances I suppose it could be true. However, it doesn't explain why we didn't have at least one success in an agency which, by industry standards, had a better than average survival rate. My conclusion, for what it is worth, is simply this—an individual needs at least three years out of college, getting his ears pinned back and acquiring some business sense in some other field before entering our business. A 25-year-old is much more mature than a 22- or 23-year-old. It is my experience that those two or three years make a world of difference in attitude and motivation, two of the key factors to success in our business.

So, for what it is worth, if I had a second chance to manage an agency I would do my level best to have the good judgment and willpower not to recruit any agents under age 25. I recommend that you consider adopting this standard unless your record of success with younger people is much better than mine. This, of course, does not preclude bringing people into the agency as trainees, where they are exposed to the agent's job with the idea that they might become attracted to it by the time they reach age 25. I was not in a position to do this or I might have considered giving it a try.

LACK OF MOTIVATION

A second weakness that I ignored too often was lack of sufficient motivation. As I have said elsewhere in this book, all motivation is self-motivation. No one ever does anything until, for whatever reason, he or she decides to do it. All of us know how much easier it is to train and supervise a motivated agent. And how difficult it is to work with one who is not.

As I look back I wonder why I hired some of the people I did when I knew, as well as I know now, how important it is in our business for an agent to be a motivated self-starter. The only explanation I have to offer is that I was so impressed with his or her other qualifications that I either ignored or failed to discover the lack of this all important quality. I can recall agents that I hired who had high test scores, excellent education backgrounds and superior markets who failed miserably. The only reason they failed was because, for some reason, they were not motivated to work at the job of selling life insurance. It would be easy to say the reason for failure was "call reluctance." But the motivated agent also has call reluctance; however, he is so motivated to be successful that he doesn't let it stop him from making the calls and seeing the people.

As I look back, the fact that the prospective agent was not sufficiently motivated to do what had to be done was probably apparent during the precontract period. The supervisor and I would discuss the agent's progress (or lack of same) and then, because he looked so good on paper, we convinced ourselves that once he came under contract things would change. But they rarely, if ever, did.

I also hired agents who gave every indication of being motivated throughout the precontract period, but when they came under contract they seemed to change and fall apart insofar as work habits were concerned. Apparently we had not hired the kind of person we thought we had.

If I had a second chance, I would do a better job of checking out each prospective recruit before bringing him or her under contract. I would spend more time discussing their qualifications with former employers and other people who knew them. I would find out as much as I could about what they had done in the past, for that is the best indication of what they will do in the future. I would try my best to find out from their past records if they could be classified as having a high degree of motivation. Furthermore, I would also strive to do a better job of evaluating a prospective agent's level of motivation during the precontract period. If it seemed apparent that they did not have it I would hope that I would have the courage to help them find other jobs.

If you believe, as I do, that it is much easier to work with and develop motivated people, I would encourage you to look for them and keep looking till you find them. They are out there and it is well worth the extra effort it takes to find them.

COMPROMISING SELECTION STANDARDS

There were other times when I compromised my selection standards. At the time I appointed a new supervisor, I often permitted him to hire a marginal recruit in order that he might have someone to work with as soon as possible. On balance, it might have served the supervisor's interests better if I had made a concerted effort to help him find a well qualified and motivated individual for his first recruit. It might not only have enabled him to get off to a better start toward building a solid unit but also have convinced him of the importance of good selection standards. On the other hand, using a true post-mortem approach, if it took us too long to find the "right" candidate, his enthusiasm and excitement for the job could be lost—perhaps permanently.

Of one thing I am certain: I never did as good a job of selection on a consistent basis as I was capable of doing. Too often I made exceptions for various reasons. I think this is true of most managers and general agents. But I am not certain that production necessarily would increase by being super selective. Turnover is better than no new agents at all. In most agencies the production from agents who did not make it is fairly significant. I know it was in mine. And we cannot ignore the fact that some agents with less than outstanding qualifications do become successful.

If I had a second chance, however, I would be more selective, as I have indicated above. But I would not overdo it. I would try to use good judgment on when to "hold them" and when to "fold them"—when to take a chance and when to be conservative.

STAYING WITH FAILURES

Another mistake I made on a fairly consistent basis was to stay too long with agents who were destined to fail. We all know that just about all agents who are truly successful get off to a fast start. There are exceptions, but in my experience they are minimal. The only rationalization I have, looking backward, for doing this, when I knew the odds were against me, was my unwillingness to admit I had made a mistake. Those who know me well are aware that I am a bit of a competitor, as I am sure most of my readers are. I guess I just did not want to give up, even though on many occasions the handwriting was definitely on the wall. When I did this I found out one of two things generally happened—neither good: I either increased my financing loss or I helped a low producer survive.

If I had it to do over again, I would strive to do a better job of early post-selection. When the manager manages to help an agent survive who probably should have been terminated early in his career, chances are he ends up with a low-producing agent. Furthermore, think of how much more profitable it would have been to have spent that time upgrading another associate who had the potential of becoming an outstanding producer.

There is another factor to be considered and that is the negative influence low producers have on the atmosphere and morale in an agency. It has often been said that "you cannot attract ducks using buzzards for decoys." That's still as valid as ever. Low producers are expensive to the company as well as the agency. I believe that early realistic post-selection on a consistent basis would reduce substantially the number of low producers in the industry.

If I had a second chance I would definitely use post-selection more intelligently. I am convinced, as I look back on my years as a manager, that my supervisors and I wasted countless hours working with agents who, for various reasons, had limited potential. If, instead, we had spent that same time with motivated associates who were capable of substantial production, the agency's results would have increased dramatically through the years.

TOO MUCH LOYALTY

In the chapter on leadership where I discuss loyalty and how important it is, I made the observation that it might be possible for the manager to be too loyal. Let me explain what I meant by telling you about an unusual situation in my agency.

It all started when we hired a young man on the basis of a referral from the Equitable of New York manager in Seattle. He was age 25 and was not a college graduate. (At the time the Equitable had a home office rule that a college degree was mandatory for appointment.) The Equitable manager was impressed with the young man and wanted to help him, so he referred him to me. Except for the lack of a college education he was a well qualified recruit.

His first year he produced well in excess of $1,000,000 of permanent life insurance at a time when that was outstanding for a first-year agent. His production continued to increase and in his third year his production was in excess of $2,000,000. By this time he was married and was the father of a young daughter. I had sponsored him for my country club and played golf with him occasionally. He was a very likable young man and appeared to have a great future ahead of him.

I cannot recall the exact sequence by which he managed to make a mess of his life, but he succeeded in doing so more completely than anyone else I have ever known. To be specific, it is my belief that there are six different types of problems an agent can have (or anyone for that matter)—financial, physical, emotional, mental, marital, and extra-marital. There may be others but this list includes most of them. Would you believe that this agent had all of them at the same time? I won't give you the details; I'll leave that to your imagination. But I assure you he had all six and was still continuing to write business.

From a post-mortem perspective it is easy to conclude that I should have recognized at some point that this guy was bad news and figured out a way to terminate him myself before the roof fell in. But I liked him, he had been a good producer and I was confident, if I could help him get his life straightened out, he could make an outstanding contribution to the agency. I am sure you have already guessed what happened. Over a period of several months the home office caught him in numerous irregularities of varying significance, primarily because of a desperate need for money. Pointing out all of his problems I defended him as best I could, and the company let him keep his contract because of my strong recommendation. But it wasn't long before they discovered some additional violations of a more flagrant nature and they immediately fired him.

Many of you may have had a similar experience of being loyal to an associate when he was in trouble—and then being made to look foolish, as I was. If I had to deal with this particular case again I hope I would exercise better judgment. But there was some positive reaction within the agency. Several other agents came to me after the story was out and said in effect, "Lew, it makes me feel more secure when I observe how you went to bat for ____________. If you would do that for a guy as messed up as he was, I know I can count on you if ever I needed you!"

It seems to me that this illustrates the fact that it is possible for a manager to be too loyal—or maybe more precisely blindly, and perhaps stupidly, loyal. I believe that would describe my conduct. In other words, I permitted my personal feelings to interfere with my judgment.

LACK OF PERSISTENCY

My agency never did have a consistent record of persistency of business in which I could take pride. I don't know exactly why this was true, but more than likely it was because I did not work at it as diligently as I should. Perhaps there was not sufficient emphasis on persistency in my compensation plan to attract my attention. Whatever the reason, I didn't do a very good job in this part of running an agency.

In the early years when we recruited as many as 28 agents in a single year, our persistency was adversely affected by those new agents. Our production grew at a rapid pace but I'm afraid we did not give conservation a very high priority. During the middle years our persistency record was better. We were not hiring as many agents, the agency was maturing and the quality of our business was much improved. In recent years when replacement became a problem our persistency record deteriorated. Over my 30 years as manager there were not very many good years insofar as persistency is concerned.

As I have indicated elsewhere in this book, it is very important for a manager to understand his contract. He should have a clear understanding of the various factors that affect his compensation, including persistency, and then make a concerted effort in those areas which are most profitable. Good persistency is much more profitable for Prudential managers under their current contract so, if I had a second chance, good judgment would indicate I should do a more effective job in this area.

Something I did which may have been a mistake was to assign my personal policyholders to agents in the agency for service and future sales when I became deeply involved in association work at the national level. I didn't feel I could give them the service they deserved. Prior to then I had produced a modest amount of business personally. However, after giving up my policyholders, my personal production was limited to the odd case which I fell into and generally I would bring an associate into the case and either split it or give it all to him.

WRITING PERSONAL BUSINESS

I started my career as an agent for two years and a personally producing supervisor for two years. In each of these four years I was the leading producer in the agency. Granted the production record was not great by today's standards, but it did give me confidence that I could enhance my management income with personal commissions, if the need arose, when I became a manager. The need was there during my early years and I found it enjoyable and profitable to write personal business on a fairly consistent basis. During this period I was undoubtedly at the peak of my personal effectiveness in the sales process. After I gave up my policyholders and, for the most part, personal selling, I found myself gradually thinking and acting less like a salesman of life insurance and more and more like a manager.

I am not suggesting that this was all bad. The record would seem to indicate that by concentrating on my managerial responsibilities only I was able to achieve a fair amount of success. Whether I could have done as well at building an agency while still maintaining a volume of personal production is a question which will never be answered. Furthermore, in retrospect, I have no regrets for having made the decision I did.

However, it may well be that if I were a manager today I would feel encouraged to write a fair volume of personal business. The marketplace has changed dramatically and it continues to change almost on a daily basis as new products and new merchandising methods are introduced. It would seem that the only way a manager can have an accurate concept of what is going on out there is to have some field involvement himself. He probably would not have to produce at MDRT level to have a feeling for what his agents were experiencing on a daily basis. A substantial case or two a month with some variety in the product mix and type of prospect would probably be adequate. It is my understanding that more and more companies are not only encouraging managers to produce but many companies, which at one time did not allow it, are now promoting it. I suspect the reasons for the switch are about the same as I have mentioned above.

There are numerous other areas of agency management where I'm sure I could have done a better job. But if we become too critical of ourselves at any stage of our careers, psychologists tell us it becomes counterproductive. We must never lose sight of the fact that managing an agency is an art; it cannot be reduced to a science. It is difficult to define what is black and what is white; there are many gray areas, as we all know, particularly when we are dealing with people.

And, lest my comments about what I might have done differently lead you to think that I am not pleased with my career, rest assured that I am. The business has been very good to me. But patting one's self on the back is, in my judgment, no way to help others reach the pinnacle.

* * *

10.

PLANNING FOR RETIREMENT

> Planning for retirement is not only essential but should be started at least by the age of 50.
> —*Robert B. Pitcher, CLU,*
> *before the Research Agencies Group in May, 1970*

I was 52 when I heard Bob Pitcher's talk, and my retirement plans were unformed. So I started thinking. One of the results of my thoughts was to join with the Life Insurance Marketing and Research Association staff (particularly Dottie Murphy, associate scientist in the research information unit) in a survey to collect some real facts from those of my colleagues who had retired, or who planned to in the reasonably near future, and to report them to the same Research Agencies Group.

We received 85 completed questionnaires from former general agents or managers who had retired, and 94 from those who were 55 or older but still active. This was an 80% response, and LIMRA people told me it was phenomenal.

Between Bob Pitcher's 1970 study and mine in 1979, we discovered that a lot of old wives' tales about retirement and plans for it—at least among general agents and managers of life insurance companies—weren't true at all. I will describe some of these, but I will not go into a great many of the statistics of the research. They are all available from LIMRA and have little place in this book. For example:

When agency managers retire, they may think of traveling a great deal. But if they were only modestly active in travel before retirement, they may find it hard work as they become older. Extensive participation in it may not be for them; after one extended trip, staying home has a great deal of appeal, even though traveling was at the top of their agenda.

Or take golf. People tend to enjoy doing what they do reasonably well. If the retiree has been a sporadic "hacker" through his working years, he does not easily adjust to a steady diet of golf, even though it sounded like a great idea when he was active in his agency. Similarly with tennis. And even with a hobby like woodworking or stamp-collecting. If he hasn't been doing it on a consistent basis prior to retirement, many times after a few months he becomes bored. It sounded like a great idea when he didn't have time to do it. Now that he does, it isn't all that appealing on a regular basis.

WHAT RETIRED AGENCY HEADS SAID

So it's evident that retirement takes more planning than conventional wisdom dictates. Most respondents to our survey thought they had undertaken such planning, but reflection taught them they could have done more. They must have looked forward to retirement—56% of them stepped down before the mandatory retirement age. But it still took them time to adjust to the new atmosphere of permissiveness and relaxation that they had never known before in their adult lives.

Why did most of them opt for early retirement? Pressure, chiefly—meeting the increasing demands of the home office for manpower and production. And if this was true five years ago among our respondents, think what it must be like today, with companies being forced to demand higher standards almost yearly.

In nine out of 10 cases, the transition in the agency was made smoothly. The retiree knew who his successor was going to be and had participated in the selection. Half the companies involved were not very helpful; only a third gave their general agents or managers any financial counselling. No company involved in the survey offered its retirees any seminars or workshops before retirement, although they agreed they could have used counselling. (In fairness to the companies, this was probably caused by the fact that at that time turnover was insufficient for a planned program. But this didn't lessen the retirees' wish for better financial counselling.)

It was chiefly the agency manager and his spouse who planned for the future, usually on an amateur basis using their native wit. More than half of them "retired into personal production in order to service their large group of clients," as the press releases always say. This, of course, in addition to the renewals and earned pension, gave their retirement better balance than a salaried employee could expect. And the lack of pressure on them was apparently one of their greatest treasures.

Almost unanimously, my group of respondents are enjoying their retirement years once they succeeded in sorting out the problems they encountered. I asked the LIMRA people if they could be saying that because they thought they ought to; the reply was that such an overwhelming preponderance, expressed so eloquently, left little room for doubt that they were telling it as it is. If one had to find a two-word reason for their pleasure in retirement, it would boil down to this: no pressure. It was expressed in many ways, but that's the sum of it.

We asked, if they could make one realistic improvement in their retirement what would it be? The top reply was, "Sufficient income to offset the effects of inflation." A good number seemed to feel ignored by their companies after retirement, and were unhappy about it—a normal reaction for proud people. Here are eight of their recommendations to their colleagues who will retire one day:

- Find an interest that you enjoy to keep you busy and provide a continuing challenge.

- Plan exactly what you will be doing come retirement day. Retire *to* something, not *from* something.

- Give thought to the possibility of disability—limited or full—and have alternatives available, if and when needed.

- Plan to be busy, but do the things you have dreamed of in an organized manner.

- Start planning many years before retirement. Plan so that your income will enable you to maintain your standard of living, if at all possible.

- Don't turn your back on everything and just move to a warm retirement community. Keep busy wherever you decide to settle down, whether by selling life insurance, doing community work or maintaining contacts with old friends.

- If you decide to move, try to sample your new way of life for a time before you make an irrevocable change.

- Three to five years ahead of time, take an exceedingly careful look in depth at retirement. Put down on paper an inventory of your assets, your outlook on life, and what you see lies ahead for you and yours. Start getting used to the facts of the idea, not just the fancies.

It's also interesting to discover what our respondents *don't* do. From 20% to 30% spent no time at all in *one* of the following activities: traveling, sports, "leisure," visiting family or friends, church activities, income-producing work and hobbies. In other words, retired agency managers have some strong ideas about what they do and don't want.

GENERAL AGENTS STILL WORKING

There are some significant differences between the agency managers who had retired at the time of the survey, and those who were still on the job. Here are some of them, which seem to point the way to an increasingly thoughtful interest on the part of the companies:

- Nearly 60% of the companies involved in an agency manager's prospective retirement took strong steps to see that a competent successor would be installed. This ranged from a purely informal agreement to a successor general agent program. Companies which have formal programs of transition start them from two to five years before the assumed date of retirement.

- General agents who are still active but on the verge of retirement report that today companies are more helpful in counselling them on retirement plans than they were even a few years ago. This ranged from individual counselling to workshops held at company meetings.

- Despite increased company activity, general agents and managers would be glad to accept an even stronger program of preparation, beginning as much as 10 years before retirement. It comes as no surprise that they would also appreciate a better pension plan to provide them with adequate retirement income.

- According to the agency heads surveyed, the most realistic help in planning for retirement was given them by their business colleagues who had already retired: "They answered my questions and pointed out mistakes they and their friends had made." Spouses and attorneys were also considered valued sources of information.

- Two-thirds of the agency heads in line for retirement had resumed personal selling or had never stopped it, and were planning to continue it upon retirement.

In almost all ways, general agents and managers contemplating retirement had the same advice for neophytes that retirees had. However, they did focus on one issue that retirees had already presumably solved: preparing for the problem of giving up command of the agency. This is not only a financial and spiritual experience; it also makes demands on the ego, and should be prepared for as thoroughly as any other element.

THE MATTER OF STRESS

"Being relieved of stress" is certainly one of the joys of retirement, among both those who have stepped down and those who are contemplating it. But stress is a complicated force, and being instantly relieved of it has its dangers.

For many years Dr. Hans Selye, the world famous medical scientist, documented the devastating effects of prolonged stress, and expressed the conviction that its effects were invariably harmful. But recently Dr. Selye announced that he had changed his mind. He now maintains that the image of stress is undeserved, and that the public and medical professionals alike have emphasized its dangers, while ignoring its positive aspects.

He now points out that there are two kinds of stress: "eustress" (the Greek prefix means "good"), which is a positive force that adds excitement and challenge to our lives, and distress, which receives all the attention.

Dr. Selye says, "There are two kinds of people: turtles and racehorses. A turtle will never run like a racehorse, and if he does he will only kill himself. But a racehorse *must* run, or he will suffer, too. The important thing is to run in the direction *of his choice.* If he does that, he'll be fine."

I suspect that most of us are familiar with people who lived only a relatively short time after they retired, even though many of them were in good health at retirement. In many of these instances, Dr. Selye's theory may well have been substantiated. When the racehorse type tries to cultivate the life-style of the turtle, spending most of his time taking it easy, his system may not accept it. Conversely, when the turtle type retires and begins to pursue a hectic life of, say, travel or sports, perhaps it may prove to be his downfall physically.

Since most general agents and managers I have known are by nature racehorses—or became so in the highly competitive business of agency management—Dr. Selye's theory dictates that they should neither spend their retirement in what Warren Harding called "innocuous desuetude" or devote all of their waking hours to becoming scratch golfers. As in most things, moderation would appear to be the answer.

HOW YOUNT DID IT

When I made my talk to the Research Agencies in '79, I concluded by boldly stating what I was going to do in almost every area you could think of. As I re-read that talk now, I believe I did so—although I will not bore you by reciting my statements here. What I had done was to take advantage of Bob Pitcher's report and what the respondents said in my own survey.

I told my wife, Grace, about Dr. Selye's theory, and she replied, "You've certainly never looked to me like a turtle." So I have become a slower racehorse, not aspiring to the Kentucky Derby but never plodding.

I have done one thing that I strongly recommend to you: I have kept a warm interest in the business to which I devoted most of my adult life. I attend NALU conventions, LAMP meetings and Research Agencies meetings. I continue to read the important periodicals of the business, and I never miss a chance to get together with my old cronies.

Here are some other suggestions that have come out of my personal experience and research (some an echo of what our respondents said):

- As your retirement date appears over the horizon, plan explicitly to get away to a flying start. Don't sag into it. We took a long and pleasurable automobile trip, thus tearing away from the routine and at the same time getting totally out of the hair of our successors. This kind of vacation might not appeal to you, but enter enthusiastically into the one that does.

- Give some thought to the possibility of disability. Keep up your customary plans for health: exercise, diet, and a positive mental attitude. As an insurance person, make sure that you have top-of-the-line "medigap" coverage so that if illness should strike, how to pay for it won't be one of your woes.

- Do the things you have dreamed of doing, but in an organized manner. I have had my activities for every day and week pretty well planned, whether they be new adventures or more mundane matters. We have done considerable travelling, including a recent trip to India, and have plans to do more.

- Start planning many years in advance for retirement, including enough income to maintain your standard of living. For insurance people, this may seem like "physician, heal thyself" advice. Yet I have seen some ex-agency manager's programs that were nowhere as thoughtfully prepared as the ones he had set up for his own clients. And you should keep in mind that while inflation has tempered in the past couple of years, it's still there and must be coped with, even if all your funds are of a variable nature.

- Don't turn your back on everything and "move to Florida," as the saying goes. This is not to say that you shouldn't have a cold weather retreat, as we have in Escondido. But, during good weather, keep busy in your own home town. We still maintain a close relationship with our friends in the church, our golfing friends and our business friends. We've known them all for more than 20 years. We feel it would be unnatural to give them up.

- Try as nearly as possible to "sample" any new way of life you may determine on before you retire and before you make a final move. We spent several vacations in Escondido, which is a resort community 30 miles north of San Diego, before we retired. We attended church there and liked both the church and the minister. We found old colleagues nearby, including some golfing buddies. People who retire to a new community "cold," or have had only a passing acquaintance with it, can be in for a shock.

- Finally—and if this is repetitive it's certainly the most important element and bears repeating as much as possible—look at retirement several years in advance and do an inventory of everything that will affect you. This includes your outlook on life as well as the more mundane concerns of assets and income.

We can't look to the great masters of the past for any sage advice about retirement, because it is peculiarly a 20th century phenomenon. Only Hugh Downs, the eminent telecaster, has said words that seem pertinent to our own future. On discussing plans for celebrating his 100th birthday, he said:

"Of course, I'm not sure that I'll be around for my 100th birthday anniversary. That's why I'm planning it. Anything we are sure of doesn't need planning. I don't plan a celebration of tomorrow's sunrise, because I am sure the sun will rise.

"When I was 20, I planned to celebrate my 21st birthday. I couldn't be sure I'd be around for *it.* But since it was a reasonable hope, I planned for it. Reaching a full century may not be as reasonable a hope, but if I don't make it, it will be because I got too sick or had too bad an accident. It won't be because I got too old. Indeed, it will be because I didn't get old enough!"

I see no reason why I shouldn't be as optimistic as Hugh Downs, so I too am planning my 100th birthday party, and I'm looking forward to having each of you accept my invitation to attend. And, incidentally, I'd be glad to come to yours if you will have me.

* * *

Here are some of the major organizations and professional associations, many of which have been referred to in this book. Contact them for more information.

The American College
270 Bryn Mawr Avenue
Bryn Mawr, Pennsylvania 19010
215/896-4500

American Council of Life Insurance (ACLI)
1850 K Street, NW
Washington, DC 20006
202/862-4000

American Society of Chartered Life Underwriters (ASCLU)
270 Bryn Mawr Avenue
Bryn Mawr, Pennsylvania 19010
215/896-4300

Association for Advanced Life Underwriting (AALU)
1922 F Street, NW
Washington, DC 20006
202/331-6081

General Agents and Managers Conference (GAMC/LAMP)
1922 F Street, NW
Washington, DC 20006
202/331-6088

International Association for Financial Planning (IAFP)
5775 Peachtree Dunwoody Road, NE
Atlanta, Georgia 30342
404/252-9600

Life Insurance Marketing and Research Association (LIMRA)
P.O. Box 208
Hartford, Connecticut 06141
203/677-0033

Life Office Management Association (LOMA)
100 Colony Square
Atlanta, Georgia 30361
404/892-7272

The Life Underwriter Training Council (LUTC)
1922 F Street, NW
Washington, DC 20006
202/393-5240

Million Dollar Round Table (MDRT)
2340 River Road
Des Plaines, Illinois 60018
312/298-1120

National Association of Life Underwriters (NALU)
1922 F Street, NW
Washington, DC 20006
202/331-6000